America Hurrah and Other Plays

Also by Jean-Claude van Itallie:

The Playwright's Workbook

Chekhov, the Major Plays (translator)

The Tibetan Book of the Dead for Reading Aloud

America Hurrah
and
Other Plays

JEAN-CLAUDE VAN ITALLIE

with an Introduction by
Bill Coco

Grove Press
New York

Eat Cake, Bag Lady, and *The Traveler* have been slightly revised
by the author for this edition.

Published simultaneously in Canada
Printed in the United States of America

FIRST EDITION

Library of Congress Cataloging-in-Publication Data
van Itallie, Jean Claude, 1936–
    America hurrah, and other plays / Jean-Claude van Itallie ; with an
introduction by Bill Coco.
        p. cm.
Contents: War—America hurrah—The serpent—Eat cake—Bag lady—
The Tibetan book of the dead, or How not to do it again—The traveler.
    ISBN 0-8021-3761-X
    I. Title.
PS3572.A45 A6 2001
812'.54—dc21
00–051399

Grove Press
841 Broadway
New York, NY 10003

01 02 03 04   10 9 8 7 6 5 4 3 2 1

CONTENTS

INTRODUCTION

This collection of Jean-Claude van Itallie's plays represents a generous overview of a twenty-five-year span in the career of one the foremost and most original American playwrights of the last half-century. His dramatic themes and forms are unusually distinctive, ranging from intense monologues that uncover the dark comedy of American consumer culture, to panoramic explorations of ancient biblical stories and Eastern wisdom. He is preoccupied with multiple levels of experience—the mask behind the mask—and states of awareness that lend a different optic to our everyday personal, political, and spiritual lives. We might think of him as a champion of late-twentieth-century American surrealism, a master of the dynamic clash of word and image.

From the start of his life, van Itallie has often been positioned to witness and record the twentieth century's complex realities. Born in 1936 into a nonpracticing Jewish family in Brussels, he fled with his family from the Nazi invasion of Belgium, disembarking in New York City in late 1940. Surely, the intense awareness of mortality that lies at the heart of nearly every van Itallie play is born of this experience.

Van Itallie grew up during the forties and fifties in the safe, prosperous, and, as he calls it, "death-denying suburb" of Great Neck, Long Island. The future playwright spoke French at home and English at school, which he says honed his interest in words and led him to understand that "reality is not contained in any single language."

Van Itallie attended Harvard, where he acted in, wrote, and directed plays, and where he came out. Then, in 1958, van Itallie came to Greenwich Village. There he studied acting at the Neighborhood Playhouse and film at NYU, wrote plays including *War* and *Motel,* and supported himself by writing cultural and religious programs for commercial television.

In the early 1960s the exciting Village "downtown theater scene" was coalescing. Rejecting fifties values and received theatrical forms, it was to blossom into the seminal off-off Broadway movement. This theatrical revolution was in fact occurring in all the arts, and we can look back on the 1960s as a kind of Golden Age of American theater. The explosion of themes and forms, with each art igniting the other, led to the invention of "happenings," "ensemble pieces," and "experimental theater." The creative anarchy in the arts of this period, heralded by Allen Ginsberg's *Howl,* reflected the social turbulence of its time—a time of radical hope (the civil rights victories, the sexual revolution) and radical darkness (the political assassinations). It was also a time of radical struggle, when the United States seemed to want to own the world and went to war in Vietnam to get it.

The deepest sources for American theatrical expression of this time can be found in the avant-garde drama of post–World War Two Europe—the "existential," or, as some say, "absurdist" French theater of Beckett, Ionesco, Genet—and in the epic theater of Brecht. The cinema was a strong force too: the experiments of Godard and Truffaut, and the dreamworks of Fellini, Antonioni, and Bergman. Later in the decade came the appearance on Broadway of Peter Brook's epochal production of *Marat/Sade* and the startling Laboratory Theater of Jerzy Grotowski.

The year 1963 holds a special significance for van Itallie: it was the year he became ensemble playwright with Joseph Chaikin's newly founded Open Theater; and the year that saw his first produced play, *War,* on the boards at the Barr-Albee-Wilder Workshop Theater on Vandam Street in the West Village. Van Itallie describes *War* as "a formal war game, a duel" between two male actors—one older, one younger—who sometimes change into father and son. There is competition and sexual tension between them. During their theatrical improvisations in the elder actor's loft, they are interrupted by a charming lady in Edwardian dress who addresses them as her children and takes them for a walk in a European park in May. At the end the kneeling men, punching each other rhythmically, form the emblem of a two-headed eagle of war, the lady blithely twirling her parasol behind them. Here, at the very beginning of his career, we can observe the roots of van Itallie's preoccupation with the personal origins of social conflict.

War was next performed off-off Broadway at the Caffe Cino, and several van Itallie plays premiered at Ellen Stewart's Café LaMama. The plays van Itallie developed and wrote for the Open Theater were performed in downtown theaters on Monday nights. These early van Itallie plays, in terms of their brevity, wit, and social commentary, resemble the early one-acts of Ionesco, or, better, Chekhov. Van Itallie's crystalline perceptions give rise to complex modes of characterization, a concern with time, and sometimes a montage approach to dramatic activity and language.

Van Itallie's most important and successful contribution as the "revolutionary playwright of the 1960s" came with the award-winning off-Broadway production of his trilogy of one-act plays (*Interview, TV,* and *Motel*) entitled *America Hurrah,* which opened at the Pocket Theatre on lower Third Avenue in November 1966. *America Hurrah,* despite or partly because of its anti-Vietnam war stance and innovative dramatic forms, was a huge, unprecedented (and unexpected by van Itallie) critical and commercial off-Broadway success. It became a cultural landmark, the watershed play of the sixties. In his *New York Times* review Walter Kerr wrote: "I think you'll be neglecting a whisper in the wind if you don't look in on *America Hurrah,* three views of the USA. There is something afoot here. . . . Mr. van Itallie treads gently across the sorrowing inattentive earth." Robert Brustein wrote in *Plays and Players:* "The American theater takes three giant steps toward maturity. . . . [van Itallie] has discovered the truest poetic function of the theatre . . . to invent metaphors which can poignantly suggest a nation's nightmares and afflictions." And Norman Mailer wrote, "It is possible *Motel* is the best one-act play I have ever seen." *America Hurrah* ran for two years off-Broadway and was acclaimed at the Royal Court Theatre in London. In Sydney, Australia, after the play's first performance a cheering audience formed a barricade to prevent vice officers from arresting the actors (because of the graffiti in *Motel*).

Interview, a fugue for eight actors, originally written for the Open Theater and first performed at Café LaMama, is a rhythmic weaving of ritualized daily behavior and speech that starts and concludes in the anonymous offices of an employment agency where all the applicants are named Smith.

TV dramatizes the menace and trivializing power of the mass media, with a trio watching television in the viewing room of a television-ratings company. The television images progressively break free of the set and eventually engulf the trio of onstage viewers.

Motel, a masque for three dolls, unfolds within a tacky Midwest motel room. (The puppets for the original LaMama production and at the Pocket Theatre were made by Robert Wilson.) A larger-than-life Motel-Keeper Doll spews forth an increasingly staccato monologue about the room and its furnishings, which are the mail-order-catalogue surface of a violent America. As she talks, the larger-than-life Man Doll and Woman Doll enter the motel room, scrawl graffiti on the walls, tear the room apart, tear the Motel-Keeper Doll apart, and march out through the audience, brandishing the Motel Keeper's limbs, while a siren wails loudly.

The culmination of the van Itallie/Chaikin Open Theater collaborations was *The Serpent.* Working with the Open Theater gave van Itallie the opportunity to discover and develop his talent as playwright for an ensemble. In director Joseph Chaikin's creative use of the workshop process to express his philosophical and political concepts, he challenged van Itallie to create new forms of play and test the limits of theatrical representation.

In creating *The Serpent,* the actors, writer, and director (helped by other artists, including Joseph Campbell who gave a lecture to the Open Theater on the mythology of the serpent) explored what myths most deeply influenced their lives. *The Serpent* opened to critical acclaim in Rome in 1967, followed by successful performances elsewhere in Europe, in New York, and throughout the United States. In *The Serpent'*s sophisticated interplay of layered actions, contemporary violence is linked to its ancient sources and seen as a central aspect of the human condition. As it simultaneously presents and confronts the values in its story, this "ceremony" for actors explores the themes and events of Genesis. The Tree of Life is a tangle of men who embody the serpent. God's fixing of limits upon Adam and Eve is humanity's projection of its own need for limits. The self-consciousness that results from the Fall leads to Cain murdering Abel, and to the unending human battle in which each of us is "caught between the beginning and the end," unable to remake the past. In a review of the downtown scene in 1971, Harold Clurman called *The Serpent* "perhaps the best single [ensemble] piece that the avant-garde theater has as yet produced in the U.S."

Since 1946, van Itallie's father had owned an old farm in western Massachusetts, and in the sixties van Itallie started to go there, sometimes with the Open Theater troupe, to write plays. In 1968, with the success of *America Hurrah,* van Itallie purchased the farm, which remains his home. It is here that in the seventies he translated his luminous and frequently produced versions of the four masterpiece dramas of Anton Chekhov. "I did my work as a playwright backwards," van Itallie has said, "creating new theatrical forms in the sixties, and in the seventies going back to study masters like Chekhov." Perhaps because in his work methods van Itallie practices his belief that "the theater is more about the spoken than the written word," the clear and poetic language of his Chekhov versions have inspired many directors and actors to use them. On his farm too, van Itallie wrote, with *Marat/Sade* composer Richard Peaslee, the musical *King of the United States,* which van Itallie directed.

Van Itallie's other plays from the seventies include *Eat Cake,* an absurdist duet on consumerism for an attractive housewife and a suave fantasy TV salesman who violates her by forcing her to eat ever more cake.

In the seventies, too, when it seemed contact between people was fragmented by paranoia, van Itallie, along with other playwrights of his generation, found the monologue form the most congenial to indepth exploration of a character's truth. His monologue *Bag Lady,* van Itallie has written, "takes place on the streets of New York City which Clara, born in pre-Holocaust Europe, calls home. . . . She ruminates on past and present, proclaiming her sovereignty as the quintessential urbanite. She's like the city itself with all its terrors. Sometimes like a crazy Zen monk, she imagines the nuclear end of New York." (*Bag Lady* is yet another example of van Itallie's gift for the monologue. Actor Jordan Charney reflects the enthusiasm of many contemporary performers when he says, "He writes the best monologues, the best.")

In 1968 during the European tour of *The Serpent,* van Itallie went to Scotland, where he met the late Chogyam Trungpa, Rinpoche, the Tibetan lama who became his Buddhist teacher (as well as Allen Ginsberg's). Trungpa was in a large part responsible for the spread of Tibetan Buddhism in America, and founded Naropa University in Boulder, Colorado, where van Itallie has often taught. Trungpa spent several long retreats on van Itallie's farm, which he renamed Shantigar, meaning "peaceful home" in Sanskrit. Van Itallie has since transformed the farm into a nonprofit foundation for theater, meditation, and healing—Shantigar Village.

Desiring to bring together his spiritual and theater work, van Itallie wrote *The Tibetan Book of the Dead, or How Not to Do It Again,* which premiered at the La Mama Annex in 1983. In its spare poetic language, its debt to ancient text, and its use of an acting ensemble, this play resembles *The Serpent,* but its landscape lies beyond history. *The Tibetan Book of the Dead* constitutes instructions on how to live fearlessly and die the same way. The joyous La Mama production featured vigorous Tibetan-style music by Steve Gorn and Jun Maeda's brightly lit two-story-high skull out of whose eyes the multiracial, multinational ensemble cast could fall like tears. The play has become a beautifully illustrated book, *The Tibetan Book of the Dead for Reading Aloud,* and an opera with music by Ricky Ian Gordon.

The Traveler, which premiered at the Mark Taper Forum in Los Angeles in 1987 and played in London at the Almeida, marks van Itallie's bringing together of his innate experimental impulses with a more Chekhovian realism. The play is inspired by van Itallie's experience as friend to Joseph Chaikin, during Chaikin's recovery from a stroke suffered during a heart operation. In the play the love and struggle between two gay men is dramatized as part of the larger canvas of life, including illness, dream, artistic creation, and everyday family drama.

In the wide-embracing vision and technique of *The Traveler,* one can also fathom portents of the drama to come in the generation of playwrights who follow van Itallie, playwrights who have taken up the playwriting landscape pioneered by van Itallie and his peers. For the younger writers the self-consciously histrionic play with form, identity, and mask that once announced a revolution has now permanently expanded the palette of dramatic possibilities. On the cover of van Itallie's book on playwriting, *The Playwright's Workbook,* Tony Kushner pays tribute to van Itallie as "the only playwriting teacher I ever had."

Van Itallie himself now combines performance and writing in his teaching and in his plays. He teaches Healing Power of Theater workshops around the country. Since 1998 he has performed in plays he has written: in *Guys Dreamin'* and in his solo autobiographical piece *War, Sex and Dreams.* His current process of playwriting is to speak the characters aloud, dictating the script rather than first writing it down—further evidence of fresh directions in his art.

The whole of van Itallie's dramatic universe is dedicated to a process of vital experimentation through the counterpoint of language, mask, and gesture. His is a philosophy of theatrical play underscored with social critique. Central to his vision is the knowledge of exile, and above all the knowledge of the brutalities that are visited upon the self as it seeks to make its way in a world almost willfully estranged from organic life.

In its American surrealistic way, van Itallie's drama takes us back to playwrights as various as Ionesco and Chekhov, and to the classical mission of comedy: laughter, which helps us to sort ourselves out morally and to open the book of our unexpected inner complexity, whatever its darkness, and whatever measure it might bring us of hope.

Bill Coco
New York City
October 2000

WAR

Gerry Ragni, Jerome Dempsey, and Jane Lowry in *War.*

photo by Alix Jeffries

War was first performed at the Barr Albee Wilder Workshop in New York City on December 22, and 23, 1963. The actors were Gerry Ragni, Jerome Dempsey and Jane Lowry. The director was Michael Kahn. In 1964 *War* opened at the Caffe Cino in New York City, the night before the Cino burned down. In 1965 a Café LaMama production of *War,* produced by Ellen Stewart and directed by Tom O'Horgan, toured Europe and played off Broadway at the Martinique Theater on a bill entitled *Six From LaMama.*

The actual words spoken by the two actors, who have met by appointment to "improvise" for an acting class are only the topmost expression of the tension that exists between them. They are playing a formal war game, a duel. Guards are down only when the lady is present. Otherwise each of the two men is always exactly aware of the other's position in the room. Every encounter and gesture is a point scored for one or the other. There should be no attempt to make the lady from next door "realistic." She should be exquisitely dreamlike, beautiful, graceful in her movements and young. If possible her dress should be an authentic one of the Edwardian period, rather than a costume; she is a remembered ideal for the two actors and for the audience.

The play works best on a proscenium stage.

The curtain opens slowly on a loft high up in New York City. No windows are visible; the stage is lit only dimly. In the center of it a man stands, his arms slightly outstretched and moving, his head down. He wears an ornate oriental dressing gown. It is very still; there is only the barely audible sound of rock and roll from a far-off radio. Suddenly a buzzer breaks the quiet; it is loud, harsh and violent. The light wavers a bit, as if the wings of a bird were fluttering about its source. The man slowly lifts his head. He is wearing a full mask, red, with white feathers around its edge and hanging down on either side of it, like a Kabuki mask. With the man's slightest movement the dressing gown rustles. His head turns slowly from side to side, as if he were watching the circling in of a large bird. The buzzer sounds again. The man backs toward the door, presses an answering buzzer which we hear sounding far down the stairs. He returns to the center of the stage, still moving slowly, still as if in terror of an ever-approaching large bird. He touches various parts of his body, portraying a stylized agony. Running footsteps are heard on the stairs. With each flight climbed they are heard closer and louder. When they are on the point of arrival the man turns to face the door, on which there is a loud double rap before it bursts open, admitting a full volume of rock and roll and revealing a young man silhouetted by harsh light from a bulb in the hall. The young man wears a pea jacket and blue jeans. He keeps one hand in his jacket. The masked man puts his hands to his ears. The young man steps into the room, closing the door behind him. The rock and roll is reduced to its original faintness.

YOUNG MAN   The light.

The masked man goes to the door, the younger man circling out of his way, and turns on the light.

The loft could be the apartment of an eccentric person, a person who has collected too many things about him, too many precious and odd bits of paraphernalia. Or it might be, too, a corner in a vast warehouse of theatrical properties and costumes. It has enough furniture to suggest a living arrangement, but the loft is filled with the tools and weapons of playacting: masks, swords, uniforms, etc. The entire rear is curtained with an old and frayed backdrop, representing a stylized European park scene.

In the light the masked man appears less extraordinary. The young man is out of breath. He indicates the other's mask.

YOUNG MAN   Take it off.

When the other man removes his mask we see he is about fifty, a character actor.

That is spooky.

ELDER ACTOR   Couldn't you have taken it from there? I was expecting you'd take it from the moment you walked in the door.

YOUNGER ACTOR   Too spooky.

There are unusually long waits between their speeches. Both are, in their own ways, en garde—*careful and formal. They are playing a serious game.*

And then, I'm not ready.

The Younger Actor has a nice smile.

I'm all out of wind.

He knows he has a nice smile.

All those flights are very tough on a fellow.

ELDER ACTOR   Not on such a young fellow.

4

YOUNGER ACTOR   How old are you, anyway?

ELDER ACTOR   I can make the steps.

YOUNGER ACTOR   It's like climbing a mountain.

ELDER ACTOR   There are mountains too where you come from, aren't there?

YOUNGER ACTOR   Uh-uh. Out there is flat, as far as the eye can see.

ELDER ACTOR   Want a drink? (*He is taking off his robe. Under it he wears loose trousers and a shirt. The Younger Actor flops into a chair.*)

YOUNGER ACTOR   In this city you're coming and going at the same time and you don't know if it's up, down or across.

The Elder Actor is folding his dressing gown neatly.

And all the time this racket. It's quiet up here.

ELDER ACTOR   Yes.

YOUNGER ACTOR   In my pad it's not. When I lay my body down to sleep, the subway's rumbling under me, light glares through the shades, a bus makes a roar like it wants to run me over.

ELDER ACTOR   No drink? (*He pours himself a shot of whiskey and drinks it down.*)

YOUNGER ACTOR   Then the garbage trucks. The garbage trucks start to whine. At all hours there's this whining. It's too hot in my pad; hot, stale and dusty. Or else it's freezing my body to the bones. And all the time wild Indians hootin' in the streets.

ELDER ACTOR   Poor baby.

YOUNGER ACTOR   What?

ELDER ACTOR   Are you ready?

YOUNGER ACTOR (*getting up*)   'Course the air up here is thin.

ELDER ACTOR   How's the job hunt?

YOUNGER ACTOR   What's all the racket in the hall?

ELDER ACTOR   Have you found a job yet?

YOUNGER ACTOR   A radio or something, isn't it? I thought you said there'd be nobody else around.

ELDER ACTOR   Only just an old woman.

YOUNGER ACTOR   Why does she play her radio so loud?

ELDER ACTOR   She's deaf, and somewhat mad. She won't disturb us.

YOUNGER ACTOR   They say you can find anything at all in this city, excepting quiet.

ELDER ACTOR   This is about as high up and as far away as can be found. If you can take it.

YOUNGER ACTOR   Say listen, I brought you a present. Hope you like it. (*Until now he has kept his hand inside his corduroy blouse. Now he draws it out slowly. In it is a very small kitten. He caresses it, and then places it on the coffee table. The Elder Actor is fascinated, but not pleased.*)

ELDER ACTOR   What is it?

YOUNGER ACTOR   It's a kitten. I almost forgot.

ELDER ACTOR   How could you almost forget? You had it in your jacket all the time.

YOUNGER ACTOR   You like it?

ELDER ACTOR   I m not fond of cats.

YOUNGER ACTOR   It's such a small cat. "Mew," it says.

ELDER ACTOR   I don't know what to do with them.

YOUNGER ACTOR   It's a problem. Your problem.

ELDER ACTOR   Yes. (*He goes among the bric-a-brac and finds an ornate gilded cage, a miniature lion's cage.*) Would you put it inside, please?

YOUNGER ACTOR   Me?

ELDER ACTOR   I don't like touching them.

YOUNGER ACTOR   "Mew." Such a wee kitten.

ELDER ACTOR   Please.

The Younger Actor finally puts it in the cage.

> Thank you. (*He shuts the door of the cage, and gets himself another small shot of liquor.*)

YOUNGER ACTOR   Something wrong?

ELDER ACTOR   How was your luck today?

YOUNGER ACTOR (*turning away, his back to the other*)   Bad.

ELDER ACTOR   What about the agent you talked about?

YOUNGER ACTOR   It's a stinking town.

ELDER ACTOR   Can't he do anything for *you?*

YOUNGER ACTOR   Says I'm a beautiful actor.

ELDER ACTOR   He's seen you act then? I didn't know you'd actually been on the stage in this city. (*He approaches the Younger Actor by one step.*)

YOUNGER ACTOR   In acting class.

ELDER ACTOR (*coming closer*)   Oh. He came to class?

YOUNGER ACTOR   *She. She* came to class.

ELDER ACTOR   Oh, she. And from how you moved she knew you were a beautiful actor?

YOUNGER ACTOR   I was doing a scene.

ELDER ACTOR   From how you moved, from how you speak . . . from your gestures . . . from the shape of your hands. (*He is very close to the Younger Actor now. The Younger Actor still has his back to him.*)

YOUNGER ACTOR   She saw you there too.

ELDER ACTOR   Did she?

He reaches around the Younger Actor to touch the handkerchief flopping from his breast pocket. The Younger Actor whirls around with a prop pistol.

YOUNGER ACTOR (*viciously*)   She said—do you want to hear what she said?—she said, "Is that old thing still around? What's he doing here?" She said, "You can't teach new tricks to a has-been."

The Elder Actor drops his hand and takes a step back. War has been declared openly.

YOUNGER ACTOR (*spinning around*)   So are you ready now? All right?

ELDER ACTOR (*making a little mock bow with his head*)   Any time.

YOUNGER ACTOR   All right.

ELDER ACTOR   I was ready when you came up.

YOUNGER ACTOR   I guess you were, with that robe and that mask and all that mumbo jumbo with the lights off. I don't need any of that at all. Just give me a minute to stretch, get in tune.

ELDER ACTOR   Any time.

The Younger Actor walks about, looking at the properties and costumes. The Elder Actor observes him. There is the formality now between them of two duelers pacing, discussing weapons.

YOUNGER ACTOR   What is all this stuff?

ELDER ACTOR   Stuff.

The Younger Actor, fingers things, inspecting the ground.

Things. Appurtenances. Stuff. Silks. Daggers. Masks. Robes. Swords. Pistols. Clubs. Uniforms. Slippers. Brocades. Velvets.

Various properties. Old muslin. Feathers, rapiers, stilts. Powders. Paints. Various things. Take your choice.

YOUNGER ACTOR   What's this?

ELDER ACTOR   A drop. An old drop.

YOUNGER ACTOR   What's behind it?

ELDER ACTOR   Nothing at all.

YOUNGER ACTOR   (*looking behind the drop*)   Windows. (*He finds a scraggly two-pointed beard and holds it up.*) What is this thing?

ELDER ACTOR   The beard of the great Genghis Khan.

YOUNGER ACTOR   It's got lice.

ELDER ACTOR   It's served.

YOUNGER ACTOR   Nobody in the theater uses this kind of stuff anymore.

ELDER ACTOR   I like it, so it doesn't matter. Besides, you can never tell when things will be back in vogue.

The Younger Actor has found, and is putting on, an old sailor top. It is a cross between a regular sailor's blouse and the top of a child's sailor suit.

YOUNGER ACTOR   How's that, huh? (*He looks at himself in a large dressing-room glass. He sings softly as he looks at himself:*)
> Bobby Shaftoe's gone to sea,
> Silver buckles on his knee.
> He'll come back and marry me,
> Pretty Bobby Shaftoe.

The Elder Actor is watching him intently, comes a step closer.

Where's the cap?

The Elder Actor picks two hats from a pile of headgear. One is the sailor's cap; the other is a woman's hat, gray with pale roses. The door opens, and the rock and roll is louder again. The Elder Actor has both hats in his

*hands. He taunts the Younger Actor with them. This time it is the
Younger Actor who is watching, who takes a step toward the Elder. There
is a great tension between them. Suddenly the Elder Actor throws the sailor
cap to the Younger Actor and, simultaneously, with his other hand holds
the other hat behind him, where the* LADY, *who is entering at that
moment, catches it up from him. It matches her dress. Suddenly with her
entrance the European park backdrop is lit as if with soft sunlight, and the
music changes from rock and roll to a melancholy and frankly poignant
waltz such as the gay nineties French tune "Reviens." The lady, in three-
quarter time, dances gently around both men. She is young. She carries a
parasol. Her dress, apricot-colored, is one which a lady of fashion in
Edwardian days might have used for strolling in the city park on a fine day.
When she has circled the actors she stops and addresses the world in general,
the audience.*

LADY (*ecstatically*)   Warvelous and grumptious. Two silken scoops
of peach ice cream. Two *pêches melbas* bespattered with baby
halves of cherries. (*She throws a kiss to the audience.*) I adore you.
Je vous adore, mes enfants. My children, *Je vous adore, mes enfants.*
See here? 'Neath the hem of my sleeve? (*She lifts, delicately and
ever so slightly, the hem of her loose three-quarter-length sleeve.*) I have
bumpgeese. *Mes* naughtys *enfants.* When I arose from my bed
this morning, I knew it was an apricot-colored day to be filled
with delights and goodies. My toe touched the ground and I
knew. My parasol. See my parasol? (*She opens her parasol and
demonstrates how well she can twirl it.*) A morning for strolling in
the *parc.* (*She strolls. This too is a dance. The music is almost
subliminally low; it sounds something like a music box. The two actors
follow behind her, gamboling, playing. They are children in her wake.*)
A splendid morning. Bright and rosy; an apricot-colored day. A
day for doing little things, *les petites choses,* and for being oh so
very happy. A day to make a child's heart rise in the expectancy
of life. A day . . . a day for playing in the park.

*There follows a long slow-motion dance pantomime. The music is almost
but not quite inaudible. She waltzes lightly while the men do a two-step
behind her. She twirls her parasol, uses it to point at a bird in a tree. One*

of the men does not see so she taps him lightly on the head with the parasol. The men pretend they are dogs and go after the bird. She points after it as it flies away from the tree. She throws a stick, which one of the men brings back in his mouth. She laughs. She settles on a bench and tells them a story, using only gestures. The men settle at her feet and whistle their reactions. There are no words. It is a memory.

And they all lived happily ever after. Very very happily. The princess in the castle, and the handsome prince watching the parade.

The two actors clap their hands in childish delight. She rises and bows to them.

I was a great actress in my day, you know. Every man in the entire world was at my feet.

They kneel at her feet.

The whole world around, the men were kneeling and only I, only I was standing while they worshiped me. To them I was a goddess. Yes, that was how it was then. Of course, of course . . .

The rock and roll has started up again slowly.

that was before I met your father. Will you hold my hat please? One of you. (*She drops the hat between the two kneeling actors and leaves, closing the door behind her, making the rock and roll faint again.*)

ELDER ACTOR Very very happily.

They remain kneeling a moment.

LADY'S VOICE (*as she opens the door a moment again*) Children, *do* something. It's not healthy; *do* go out and play.

The door closes again. The two actors get up and, crossing each other, go to opposite sides of the stage. They are strangers on a street. They eye each other suspiciously. Street sounds are heard vaguely in the music. They walk around each other cautiously. One turns his back, and then spins to face his opponent again. They look up at a building in construction.

ELDER ACTOR   They're tearing everything down these days.

YOUNGER ACTOR   Yeah. All old stuff.

They separate. Then they come back to each other.

Ugly-looking thing. Isn't it?

ELDER ACTOR   It's a shame. Tearing down all the nice old buildings.

YOUNGER ACTOR   I meant the old building is ugly. That's what I meant.

ELDER ACTOR (*shaking his head*)   Here today, gone tomorrow.

YOUNGER ACTOR   Have you got a light?

ELDER ACTOR   Yeah, sure, Son, here.

YOUNGER ACTOR   Thanks, Dad.

The Elder Actor drops the match in annoyance and grinds it out. The Younger Actor spins away in a childish pique.

Aw, Dad. Have a heart, Dad. When *can I* smoke?

ELDER ACTOR   When you're grown up.

YOUNGER ACTOR   Can't you tell yet that a guy's grown-up yet, huh?

ELDER ACTOR   You've been smoking since you were four. That doesn't make you grown-up, and don't ask me to light your cigarettes.

YOUNGER ACTOR   I don't smoke, Dad.

They are "improvising," creating scenes from momentary inspiration.

ELDER ACTOR   What's that you've got on your head, Son?

YOUNGER ACTOR   That's a sailor cap, Dad.

ELDER ACTOR   Well don't get it dirty in the park.

YOUNGER ACTOR   I've joined the navy, Dad.

ELDER ACTOR   You can smoke when you're grown-up. When you're big.

YOUNGER ACTOR   I'm going to see the world, Dad. Like you. Like all those pictures on the subway say. Join up and see the world. Get an education. See the world. That's for me, Dad.

ELDER ACTOR   You're going to hurt me, Son. And your mother. You're going to hurt everybody.

YOUNGER ACTOR   It's my life, Dad. I've got to live it my way, Dad. Last night I took Mary Lou behind the apple tree.

ELDER ACTOR   What apple tree?

YOUNGER ACTOR   On the fire escape. She lifted her skirt, Dad. I'm going to see the world. I saw under her skirt, Dad, I want to see more. I want to see it all. I want it all for me.

ELDER ACTOR   What'd you do when Mary Lou lifted her skirt, Son?

YOUNGER ACTOR   I decided to join the navy, Dad. See the world. Get an education. Get depraved.

ELDER ACTOR   What'd you do when the slut lifted her skirt ?

The Younger Actor doesn't answer.

Give me that cap.

YOUNGER ACTOR   No.

ELDER ACTOR   I said give me that cap, Sailor. (*He takes it and puts it on his own head. Immediately his manner is more confident.*) Now. So you want to join the navy. That's what I'm here for. What're your qualifications? What've you done? (*He is now the recruiting officer.*)

YOUNGER ACTOR   When she lifted it up she giggled, and then she was quiet.

ELDER ACTOR   So much for references.

YOUNGER ACTOR   I touched it with my finger and it was moist.

ELDER ACTOR   Yes, football's a man's game. What else? It says here you played tuba in the school band. That right?

YOUNGER ACTOR   I just touched it.

ELDER ACTOR   So you didn't finish high school. That's all right. You'll get an education in the navy.

YOUNGER ACTOR   It was moist. I didn't expect that. And she breathed heavy.

ELDER ACTOR   How old are you, Son?

YOUNGER ACTOR   I used to think she was a slut too, like Dad said. She had breasts before everybody, and she went to the beauty parlor by herself. Long strawberry hair. In the gym locker room they said:

>Mary Lou, Mary Lou,
>Here's a little sou
>Open up and put it in your—

What'd she want from me?

ELDER ACTOR   Better talk it over with your mother. We don't take them underage in the U.S. Navy. Go home and have your mother wipe the snot off your nose.

YOUNGER ACTOR   It was moist, and she stopped giggling.

ELDER ACTOR   We don't take dirty depraved snotty-nosed boys.

YOUNGER ACTOR   What'd she want from me?

ELDER ACTOR   I want something from you. Come here, Boy.

The Younger Actor backs off.

Come to me, little baby. You think you've got the world all made for you, don't you? What you need is a little discipline. I'll muss up that curly-combed hair. You want to be a man, or do you just want a navy cap to make you think you're a man? Huh, Baby? What is it?

They circle each other, their arms swinging. The Elder Actor is stalking.

Come to me, Baby. I'll fix it. Little baby-faced American.

YOUNGER ACTOR   Kraut.

ELDER ACTOR   Mama can't help you now. Nigger boy.

YOUNGER ACTOR   Son of a bitch of a Chink. Come and get me if you can.

ELDER ACTOR   Baby fruitcake.

YOUNGER ACTOR   Wop. Spick. Nigger.

ELDER ACTOR   You poor little bastard. Come on, mama's boy. Afraid?

YOUNGER ACTOR   What do you want, Frog? what do you want, Mick?

ELDER ACTOR   Him got a big mouth, huh, Baby? Got a mouth like a woman. Got a mouth like a bitch.

YOUNGER ACTOR   You fairy. Fuckin' fairy.

ELDER ACTOR   Shut up, punk. We got a name for you. You're a sissy. Can't take it. A little sissy.

YOUNGER ACTOR   Okay, Stupid. Prove it, Stupid.

ELDER ACTOR   Your mother's got fleas.

YOUNGER ACTOR   Go stick your head in a barrel.

ELDER ACTOR   Crybaby.

YOUNGER ACTOR   Crybaby yourself. Go eat doody.

ELDER ACTOR   Go stick your head in a barrel.

YOUNGER ACTOR   Go stick your head in a barrel of doody.

ELDER ACTOR   You smell. You stink.

YOUNGER ACTOR   Tattletale.

ELDER ACTOR   Crybaby.

YOUNGER ACTOR   Crybaby yourself.

ELDER ACTOR   Yeah.

YOUNGER ACTOR   Yeah. Yeah.

They have regressed to near infancy, and begin to chant the war chant of the child caught impotently in his crib. They stick their tongues out at each other. The Lady returns.

LADY   Oh. Now. Oh, now. Now, now, now, now, there. No, no. Idle baby hands make for idle baby play. (*As she speaks she glides about the stage.*) You must make something. Make something of yourself for me. Make something for me, to make me happy. There now. Now, now.

They are still.

I'm out for a walk, and I want you to make me a surprise. Build me a surprise.

They start to gather large building blocks colored like bricks.

Make me a beautiful surprise.

She leaves, closing the door behind her, and they start to build. They face each other, each working on one wall. They work diligently.

YOUNGER ACTOR   What are you building?

ELDER ACTOR   A surprise. What are you building?

YOUNGER ACTOR   Mine's a surprise too. It's a palace.

They work.

Is yours a bomb?

ELDER ACTOR   Certainly not.

YOUNGER ACTOR   What's yours made of?

ELDER ACTOR   Bricks.

YOUNGER ACTOR   So is mine.

The Elder Actor is highly methodical.

ELDER ACTOR   The bricklayer's craft is complex.

YOUNGER ACTOR   And noble.

ELDER ACTOR (*wiping off a brick*)   A bricklayer must be neat and clean.

YOUNGER ACTOR   A bricklayer is a noble builder of cathedrals and skyscrapers.

The Younger Actor works fast, not too carefully.

ELDER ACTOR   I start with the quoins, or corners,

The Younger pays no attention.

which I build up eight or ten courses high. I make use of rule, square, set square, bevel, compass, level and plumb rule.

He grunts a bit with the work. The Younger Actor steps off to contemplate what little he has done.

YOUNGER ACTOR   Shall I build a palace or a skycraper? I don't know.

ELDER ACTOR   I proceed to lay the courses the length of the wall between.

YOUNGER ACTOR   I will build a skyscraper. It will soar to the sky in all the lovely colors of the rainbow, the tip of it lost in the sun, golden, twenty-four karats golden.

ELDER ACTOR   Bricks are laid with the frog uppermost always.

YOUNGER ACTOR   In it I'll have thirteen-year-old girls with strawberry hair, all in pink nighties. And crisp secretaries with no skirts.

ELDER ACTOR   Even good bricklayers again and again forget to flush up.

YOUNGER ACTOR   Just panties.

ELDER ACTOR   This is sloppy.

YOUNGER ACTOR   And inside'll be fountains and flowers and lace and marble. Some soft music. Or maybe no sound but the little hum of movie cameras catching every move I make for people all over the world to see.

ELDER ACTOR   In dry weather the bricks must be wetted. (*He picks up a brick and contemplates it with disgust.*) I don't like to dip them in buckets of water as this makes my hands wet and sore.

YOUNGER ACTOR   I'll also build a summer house by the sea, a great palace of glass and stone by the sea.

ELDER ACTOR   Therefore I sprinkle water over the bricks before they are laid.

YOUNGER ACTOR   I'll have a private gym, done in blue.

ELDER ACTOR   I carry my work up three or four feet at a time with daily regularity.

YOUNGER ACTOR   I will live forever.

ELDER ACTOR   If brickwork is carried up too quickly it settles and is out of plumb.

YOUNGER ACTOR   I will have a charge account at the florist's. (*This is his highest dream.*)

ELDER ACTOR   I am a good bricklayer. I carry up my work with daily regularity.

The Younger Actor looks at the Elder's work.

YOUNGER ACTOR   Why, that's an outhouse.

He kicks a brick off the Elder's work. The Elder Actor rises and they face each other.

ELDER ACTOR (*intently*)   Bad boy.

The Younger Actor laughs and walks off. The Elder Actor rushes to the Lady's hat and puts it on. He parades in it, a parody of the Lady. The Younger Actor is fascinated.

YOUNGER ACTOR   Excuse me.

The Elder Actor is engrossed in his promenade.

Excuse me.

ELDER ACTOR   (*as if startled*)   Oh. (*His speech is a broad burlesque of the Lady's.*)

YOUNGER ACTOR   I seem to remember you.

ELDER ACTOR   Oh, no, Sir. You must be mistaken.

YOUNGER ACTOR   I'm very sure.

ELDER ACTOR (*as if flattered*)   Are you?

YOUNGER ACTOR   I'm quite certain we were once close and dear friends.

ELDER ACTOR   It's possible of course. *C'est possible.*

YOUNGER ACTOR   Didn't you once have a parasol?

ELDER ACTOR   *C'est possible.* You know how it is in May in the park. (*He picks up a riding whip and puts it over his shoulder as a parasol.*) It either rains or it shines. And in either case a parasol is essential. (*He twirls the riding whip on his shoulder.*) Do you like it? Did you happen to notice my dress? Shocking pink with three-quarter-length sleeves. They're back in this year.
And the hat. Do you like the hat?

YOUNGER ACTOR   Oh yes. I remember the hat.

ELDER ACTOR (*singing, badly*)   "In the merry merry month of May, I was strolling through the park one day. I was taken by surprise . . . (*He ogles the Younger Actor*) . . . by a pair of roguish eyes . . .

19

(*He rolls his own eyes.*) . . . that stole my poor heart away." (*He offers his arm to the Younger Actor. Both of them sing the song through, dancing a comic and grotesque pas de deux.*)

ELDER ACTOR   Oh la, Sir. How *jolie* it was that season; all the people in all the plays had parasols. And you say you remember me? Say it again.

YOUNGER ACTOR   I could hardly mistake you, I don't think. It is one of my loveliest memories. My very loveliest in fact. Nothing else has ever touched it. I couldn't make a mistake about that. That memory lies here. (*He touches his heart.*) Deep inside me. (*He is very serious. Kneeling at the other's feet to make this declaration:*) I couldn't mistake you.

ELDER ACTOR   Oh la, Sir. Oh, look, Sir, there's a bird in that tree.

He points with the riding whip. The other looks.

YOUNGER ACTOR   Where?

ELDER ACTOR (*bashing him on the head with the riding whip*)   Right there.

YOUNGER ACTOR (*rubbing his head*)   Yes, I see it, I think.

ELDER ACTOR   What fun to frolic in the park with you. (*He pulls the Younger Actor by the hand and they skip about.*) This is my favorite role. I love myself in this role. I remember very well now.

YOUNGER ACTOR   I'm not so sure anymore.

ELDER ACTOR   Let's do it again. (*He pushes the Younger Actor into a kneeling position again. He throws the riding crop to a corner of the stage.*) Run and fetch this. Go and get it now. Go on.

The Younger Actor retrieves it on all fours. When he has brought the whip halfway back he stops.

What is it? What's the matter?

YOUNGER ACTOR   I don't think it was you after all.

ELDER ACTOR   But you said it was. Just a minute ago. Don't you remember?

YOUNGER ACTOR (*standing*)   No.

ELDER ACTOR (*frightened, clutching the hat*)   You remember the hat.

YOUNGER ACTOR   It wasn't you.

ELDER ACTOR   Gray with pink roses.

YOUNGER ACTOR (*snapping the whip*)   No.

ELDER ACTOR   Please.

YOUNGER ACTOR (*snapping the whip again*)   No. (*He snaps the whip twice more.*)

ELDER ACTOR   Mew.

YOUNGER ACTOR (*snapping it again*)   It's not the same.

ELDER ACTOR   Mew.

The Younger Actor snaps the whip again. The Elder Actor holds the hat to his body.

Mew. Mew.

YOUNGER ACTOR   It's not the same, ever. (*He breaks the whip in two and throws it away.*)

ELDER ACTOR   No. (*He drops the hat.*) It's not.

They are no longer facing each other.

It was so long ago and they lived happily ever after. Very very happily.

There is a moment when both are sad. The Lady's laugh—light, not mocking—is heard outside the door. She comes in and dances softly about them. They remain where they are, not looking at her but sensing her. Back at the door she stops.

LADY And, oh my darling, be sure and pack warm warm socks. Bow to the ladies and speak up to the gentlemen. Be a little man. You've an extra pair of socks so *don't* wear your sandals in the mud. Don't come back to me with muddy sandals. When the parade goes by, stand up straight and wave. And remember I'll be here all the time. Every day at highest noon when you look up at the sun, I'll be looking at the same sun. And in the evening of the full moon look up at eight-thirty precisely, and I'll be looking too. Be oh so good. Bring me back a little present.

There starts the sound of gunfire and explosions, which slowly builds over the music.

I can't quite hear the music anymore. But I'll be here. And every day I'll go for a walk in the park and at noon, at highest highest noon, I'll look straight at the sun, every day of my life, through my parasol. And you must be looking too. Look for me.

ELDER ACTOR Ten shot!

Both actors stand at military attention.

LADY The music is fading. Never mind. I don't mind. I really don't. I really really don't. See what a lovely day it will be. *Quelle belle journée.* (*She opens her parasol.*)

YOUNGER ACTOR Fohwahd.

LADY It may have been, it might have been, I know, the weest bit *too* wonderful in the *parc, trop beau,* but I never, I never meant you, anything but love.

YOUNGER ACTOR Harch!

The two actors, crossing by each other, march to either side of the stage.

LADY See what a lovely day it will be.

The actors are facing the audience on either side of the stage, marching in place.

LADY   *Quelle belle journée.*

*The lady brings her parasol down over her face. The sound of the actors'
shoes on the stage is loud and rythmic. The music can still be very faintly
heard behind the cannonfire and gunshot and explosions. The actors march
in toward each other. They kneel at the center of the stage. They put their
inner arms around each other but with their free arms they continue to hit
each other. The lady steps up from behind them, her face still covered by the
parasol, which is twirling, and stands above them; this tableau forms a
hieroglyph, an emblem, the two-headed eagle of war. There is silence.*

THE CURTAIN FALLS SLOWLY.

AMERICA HURRAH
(INTERVIEW, TV, MOTEL)

America Hurrah is a trilogy of three short plays: *Interview,* a fugue for eight actors; *TV;* and *Motel,* a masque for three dolls.

*America Hurra*h premiered off Broadway at the Pocket Theatre in New York City on November 7, 1966, where it ran for 640 performances, then moved to the Royal Court Theatre in London. *Interview* was directed by Joseph Chaikin. *TV* and *Motel* were directed by Jacques Levy and produced by Stephanie Sills. The cast consisted of Joyce Aaron, James Barbosa, Henry Calvert, Conard Fowkes, Ronnie Gilbert, Cynthia Harris, Bill Macy, Brenda Smiley and the voice of Ruth White. *Motel* dolls were constructed by Robert Wilson.

INTERVIEW
A FUGUE FOR
EIGHT ACTORS

photo by Phill Niblock

Interview as a single play premiered at the Café LaMama ETC, New York City, in 1964, directed by Peter Feldman.

The set is white and impersonal.

On the sides there is one entrance for Applicants and another entrance for Interviewers.

The only furniture or props needed are eight gray blocks.

The actors, four men and four women, are dressed in black and white street clothes. During the employment agency section only, Interviewers wear translucent plastic masks.

There is intermittent harpsichord accompaniment: dance variations (minuet, Virginia reel, twist) on a familiar American tune, but much of the music—singing, whistling, humming—is provided by the actors on stage. It is suggested, moreover, that as a company of actors and a director approach the play they find their own variations in rhythmic expression. The successful transition from one setting to the next depends on the actors' ability to play together as a company and to drop character instantaneously and completely in order to assume another character, or for a group effect.

The first interviewer for an employment agency, a young woman, sits on stage as the first applicant, a housepainter, a man, enters.

FIRST INTERVIEWER (*standing*)   How do you do?

FIRST APPLICANT (*sitting*)   Thank you, I said, not knowing where to sit.

The characters will often include the audience in what they say, as if the characters were being interviewed by the audience.

FIRST INTERVIEWER (*pointedly*)   Won't you sit down?

FIRST APPLICANT (*standing again quickly, afraid to displease*)   I'm sorry.

FIRST INTERVIEWER (*busy with imaginary papers, pointing to a particular seat*)   There. Name please?

FIRST APPLICANT   Jack Smith.

FIRST INTERVIEWER   Jack What Smith?

FIRST APPLICANT   Beg pardon?

FIRST INTERVIEWER Fill in the blank space, please. Jack blank space Smith.

FIRST APPLICANT I don't have any.

FIRST INTERVIEWER I asked you to sit down. (*points*) There.

FIRST APPLICANT (*sitting*) I'm sorry.

FIRST INTERVIEWER Name, please?

FIRST APPLICANT Jack Smith.

FIRST INTERVIEWER You haven't told me your *middle* name.

FIRST APPLICANT I haven't got one.

FIRST INTERVIEWER (*suspicious but writing it down*) No middle name.

Second applicant, a floorwasher, a woman, enters.

FIRST INTERVIEWER How do you do?

SECOND APPLICANT (*sitting*) Thank you, I said, not knowing what.

FIRST INTERVIEWER Won't you sit down?

SECOND APPLICANT (*standing*) I'm sorry.

FIRST APPLICANT I am sitting.

FIRST INTERVIEWER (*pointing*) There. Name, please?

SECOND APPLICANT (*sitting*) Jane Smith.

FIRST APPLICANT Jack Smith.

FIRST INTERVIEWER What blank space Smith?

SECOND APPLICANT Ellen.

FIRST APPLICANT Haven't got one.

FIRST INTERVIEWER What job are you applying for?

FIRST APPLICANT Housepainter.

SECOND APPLICANT   Floorwasher.

FIRST INTERVIEWER   We haven't many vacancies in that. What experience have you had?

FIRST APPLICANT   A lot.

SECOND APPLICANT   Who needs experience for floorwashing?

FIRST INTERVIEWER   You will help me by making your answers clear.

FIRST APPLICANT   Eight years.

SECOND APPLICANT   Twenty years.

Third applicant, a banker, enters.

FIRST INTERVIEWER   How do you do?

SECOND APPLICANT   I'm good at it,

FIRST APPLICANT   Very well.

THIRD APPLICANT (*sitting*)   Thank you, I said, as casually as I could.

FIRST INTERVIEWER   Won't you sit down?

THIRD APPLICANT (*standing again*)   I'm sorry.

SECOND APPLICANT   I am sitting.

FIRST APPLICANT (*standing again*)   I'm sorry.

FIRST INTERVIEWER (*pointing to a particular seat*)   There. Name, please?

FIRST APPLICANT   Jack Smith.

SECOND APPLICANT   Jane Smith.

THIRD APPLICANT   Richard Smith.

FIRST INTERVIEWER   What *exactly* Smith, please?

THIRD APPLICANT   Richard F.

SECOND APPLICANT Jane Ellen.

FIRST APPLICANT Jack None.

FIRST INTERVIEWER What are you applying for?

FIRST APPLICANT Housepainter.

SECOND APPLICANT I need money.

THIRD APPLICANT Bank president.

FIRST INTERVIEWER How many years have you been in your present job?

THIRD APPLICANT Three.

SECOND APPLICANT Twenty.

FIRST APPLICANT Eight.

Fourth applicant, a lady's maid, enters.

FIRST INTERVIEWER How do you do?

FOURTH APPLICANT I said, thank you, not knowing where to sit.

THIRD APPLICANT I'm fine.

SECOND APPLICANT Do I have to tell you?

FIRST APPLICANT Very well.

FIRST INTERVIEWER Won't you sit down?

FOURTH APPLICANT I'm sorry.

THIRD APPLICANT (*sitting again*) Thank you.

SECOND APPLICANT (*standing again*) I'm sorry.

FIRST APPLICANT (*sitting*) Thanks.

FIRST INTERVIEWER (*pointing to a particular seat*) There. Name, please?

Fourth applicant sits.

ALL APPLICANTS Smith.

FIRST INTERVIEWER What Smith?

FOURTH APPLICANT Mary Victoria.

THIRD APPLICANT Richard F.

SECOND APPLICANT Jane Ellen.

FIRST APPLICANT Jack None.

FIRST INTERVIEWER How many years' experience have you had?

FOURTH APPLICANT Eight years.

SECOND APPLICANT Twenty years.

FIRST APPLICANT Eight years.

THIRD APPLICANT Three years, four months and nine days not counting vacations and sick leave and the time both my daughters and my wife had the whooping cough.

FIRST INTERVIEWER Just answer the questions please.

FOURTH APPLICANT Yes, sir.

THIRD APPLICANT Sure.

SECOND APPLICANT I'm sorry.

FIRST APPLICANT That's what I'm doing.

Second interviewer, a young man, enters and goes to inspect applicants. With the entrance of each interviewer, the speed of the action accelerates.

SECOND INTERVIEWER How do you do?

FIRST APPLICANT (*standing*) I'm sorry.

SECOND APPLICANT (*sitting*) Thank you.

THIRD APPLICANT (*standing*) I'm sorry.

FOURTH APPLICANT (*sitting*) Thank you.

SECOND INTERVIEWER What's your name?

FIRST INTERVIEWER Your middle name, please.

FIRST APPLICANT Smith.

SECOND APPLICANT Ellen.

THIRD APPLICANT Smith, Richard F.

FOURTH APPLICANT Mary Victoria Smith.

FIRST INTERVIEWER What is your exact age?

SECOND INTERVIEWER Have you any children?

FIRST APPLICANT I'm thirty-two years old.

SECOND APPLICANT One son.

THIRD APPLICANT I have two daughters.

FOURTH APPLICANT Do I have to tell you that?

FIRST INTERVIEWER Are you married, single or other?

SECOND INTERVIEWER Have you ever earned more than that?

FIRST APPLICANT No.

SECOND APPLICANT Never.

THIRD APPLICANT Married.

FOURTH APPLICANT Single, *now*.

Third interviewer, a woman, enters.

THIRD INTERVIEWER How do you do?

FIRST APPLICANT (*sitting*) Thank you.

SECOND APPLICANT (*standing*) I'm sorry.

THIRD APPLICANT (*sitting*) Thank you.

FOURTH APPLICANT (*standing*) I'm sorry.

Fourth interviewer, a man, appears on the heels of third interviewer.

FOURTH INTERVIEWER   How do you do?

FIRST APPLICANT (*standing*)   I'm sorry.

SECOND APPLICANT (*sitting*)   Thank you.

THIRD APPLICANT (*standing*)   I'm sorry.

FOURTH APPLICANT (*sitting*)   Thank you.

ALL INTERVIEWERS   What is your social security number, please?

Applicants do the next four speeches simultaneously.

FIRST APPLICANT   333 dash 6598 dash 5590765439 dash 003.

SECOND APPLICANT   999 dash 5733 dash 699075432 dash 11.

THIRD APPLICANT (*sitting*)   I'm sorry. I left it home. I can call home if you let me use the phone.

FOURTH APPLICANT   I always get it confused with my checking account number.

Interviewers do the next four speeches in a round.

FIRST INTERVIEWER   Will you be so kind as to tell me a little about yourself?

SECOND INTERVIEWER   Can you fill me in on something about your background please?

THIRD INTERVIEWER   It'd be a help to our employers if you'd give me a little for our files.

FOURTH INTERVIEWER   Now what would you say, say, to a prospective employer about yourself?

Applicants address parts of the following four speeches in particular directly to the audience.

FIRST APPLICANT   I've been a union member twenty years, I said to them, if that's the kind of thing you want to know. Good health, I said. Veteran of two wars. Three kids. Wife's dead. Wife's sister, she takes care of them. I don't know why I'm telling you this, I said, smiling. (*Sits.*)

SECOND APPLICANT (*standing*) So what do you want to know, I told the guy. I've been washin' floors for twenty years. Nobody's ever complained. I don't loiter after hours, I said to him. Just because my boy's been in trouble is no reason, I said, no reason—I go right home, I said to him. Right home. (*Sits.*)

THIRD APPLICANT (*standing*) I said that I was a Republican and we could start right there. And then I said that I spend most of my free time watching television or playing in the garden of my four-bedroom house with our lovely daughters, aged nine and eleven. I mentioned that my wife plays with us, too, and that her name is Katherine, although, I said, casually, her good friends call her Kitty. I wasn't at all nervous. (*Sits.*)

FOURTH APPLICANT (*standing*) Just because I'm here, sir, I told him, is no reason for you to patronize me. I've been a lady's maid, I said, in houses you would not be allowed into. My father was a gentleman of leisure, *and,* what's more, I said, my references are unimpeachable.

FIRST INTERVIEWER I see.

SECOND INTERVIEWER All right.

THIRD INTERVIEWER That's fine.

FOURTH INTERVIEWER Of course.

Applicants do the following four speeches simultaneously.

FIRST APPLICANT Just you call anybody at the union and ask them. They'll hand me a clean bill of health.

SECOND APPLICANT I haven't been to jail if that's what you mean. Not me. I'm clean.

THIRD APPLICANT My record is impeccable. There's not a stain on it.

FOURTH APPLICANT   My references would permit me to be a governess, that's what.

FIRST INTERVIEWER (*going to first applicant and inspecting under his arms*)   When did you last have a job housepainting?

SECOND INTERVIEWER (*going to second applicant and inspecting her teeth*)   Where was the last place you worked?

THIRD INTERVIEWER (*going to third applicant and inspecting him*)   What was your last position in a bank?

FOURTH INTERVIEWER (*going to fourth applicant and inspecting her*)   Have you got your references with you?

Applicants do the following four speeches simultaneously, with music under.

FIRST APPLICANT   I've already told you I worked right along till I quit.

SECOND APPLICANT   Howard Johnson's on Fifty-first Street all last month.

THIRD APPLICANT   First Greenfield International and Franklin Banking Corporation Banking and Stone Incorporated.

FOURTH APPLICANT   I've got a letter right here in my bag. Mrs. Muggintwat only let me go because she died.

Interviewers do the next four speeches in a round.

FIRST INTERVIEWER (*stepping around and speaking to the second applicant*)   Nothing terminated your job at Howard Johnson's? No franks, say, missing at the end of the day, I suppose?

SECOND INTERVIEWER (*stepping around and speaking to the third applicant*)   It goes without saying, I suppose, that you could stand an FBI security test?

THIRD INTERVIEWER (*stepping around and speaking to the fourth applicant*)   I suppose there are no records of minor thefts, or shall we say, borrowings, from your late employer?

FOURTH INTERVIEWER (*stepping around and speaking to the first applicant*) Nothing political in your Union dealings? Nothing leftist, I suppose? Nothing rightist either, I hope.

Applicants and interviewers line up for a square dance. Music under the following.

FIRST APPLICANT (*bowing to the first interviewer*) What's it to you, buddy?

SECOND APPLICANT (*bowing to the second interviewer*) Eleanor Roosevelt wasn't more honest.

THIRD APPLICANT (*bowing to the third interviewer*) My record is lily-white, sir!

FOURTH APPLICANT (*bowing to the fourth interviewer*) Mrs. Thumbletwat used to take me to the bank and I'd watch her open her box!

Each interviewer, during his or her next speech, goes upstage to form another line.

FIRST INTERVIEWER Good!

SECOND INTERVIEWER Fine!

THIRD INTERVIEWER Swell!

FOURTH INTERVIEWER Fine!

Applicants come downstage together; they do the next four speeches simultaneously and directly to the audience.

FIRST APPLICANT I know my rights. As a veteran. *And* a citizen. I know my rights. *And* my cousin is very well-known in certain circles, if you get what I mean. In the back room of a certain candy store in the Italian district of this city my cousin is *very* well known, if you get what I mean. I know my rights. And I know my cousin.

SECOND APPLICANT (*putting on a pious act, looking up to Heaven*) Holy Mary Mother of God, must I endure all the sinners of this earth? Must I go on a poor washerwornan in this City of Sin? Help me, oh my God, to leave this earthly crust, and damn your silly impudence young fellow if you think you can treat an old woman like this. You've got another thought coming, you have.

THIRD APPLICANT   I have an excellent notion to report you to the Junior Chamber of Commerce of this City of which I am the Secretary and was in line to be elected Vice President and still will be if you are able to find me gainful and respectable employ!

FOURTH APPLICANT   Miss Thumblebottom married into the Twiths and if you start insulting me, young man, you'll have to start in insulting the Twiths as well. A Twith isn't a nobody, you know, as good as a Thumbletwat, *and* they all call me their loving Mary, you know.

ALL INTERVIEWERS (*in loud raucous voices*)   Do you smoke?

Each applicant, during his or her next speech, turns upstage.

FIRST APPLICANT   No thanks.

SECOND APPLICANT   Not now.

THIRD APPLICANT   No thanks.

FOURTH APPLICANT   Not now.

ALL INTERVIEWERS (*again in a harsh voice and bowing or curtsying*)   Do you mind if I do?

FIRST APPLICANT   I don't care.

SECOND APPLICANT   Who cares?

THIRD APPLICANT   'Course not.

FOURTH APPLICANT   Go ahead.

Interviewers form a little group off to themselves.

FIRST INTERVIEWER   I tried to quit but couldn't manage.

SECOND INTERVIEWER   I'm a three-pack-a-day man, I guess.

THIRD INTERVIEWER   If I'm gonna go I'd rather go smoking.

FOURTH INTERVIEWER   I'm down to five a day.

Applicants all start to sneeze.

FIRST APPLICANT   Excuse me, I'm gonna sneeze.

SECOND APPLICANT   Have you got a hanky?

THIRD APPLICANT   I have a cold coming on.

FOURTH APPLICANT   I thought I had some tissues in my bag.

Applicants all sneeze.

FIRST INTERVIEWER   Gezundheit.

SECOND INTERVIEWER   God bless you.

THIRD INTERVIEWER   Gezundheit.

FOURTH INTERVIEWER   God bless you.

Applicants all sneeze simultaneously.

FIRST INTERVIEWER   God bless you.

SECOND INTERVIEWER   Gezundheit.

THIRD INTERVIEWER   God bless you.

FOURTH INTERVIEWER   Gezundheit.

Applicants return to their seats.

FIRST APPLICANT   Thanks, I said.

SECOND APPLICANT   I said thanks.

THIRD APPLICANT   Thank you, I said.

FOURTH APPLICANT   I said thank you.

Interviewers stand on their seats and say the following as if one person were speaking.

FIRST INTERVIEWER Do you

SECOND INTERVIEWER speak any

THIRD INTERVIEWER foreign

FOURTH INTERVIEWER languages?

FIRST INTERVIEWER Have you

SECOND INTERVIEWER got a

THIRD INTERVIEWER college

FOURTH INTERVIEWER education?

FIRST INTERVIEWER Do you

SECOND INTERVIEWER take

THIRD INTERVIEWER shorthand?

FOURTH INTERVIEWER Have you

FIRST INTERVIEWER any

SECOND INTERVIEWER special

THIRD INTERVIEWER qualifications?

FIRST INTERVIEWER Yes?

FIRST APPLICANT (*stepping up to interviewers*) Sure, I can speak Italian, I said. My whole family is Italian so I oughta be able to, and I can match colors, like green to green, so that even your own mother couldn't tell the difference, begging your pardon, I said, I went through the eighth grade. (*Steps back.*)

SECOND INTERVIEWER Next.

SECOND APPLICANT (*stepping up to interviewers*) My grandmother taught me some Gaelic, I told the guy. And my old man could rattle off in Yiddish when he had a load on. I never went to school at all excepting church school, but I can write my name

41

good and clear. Also, I said, I can smell an Irishman or a Yid a hundred miles off. (*Steps back.*)

THIRD INTERVIEWER   Next.

THIRD APPLICANT (*stepping up to interviewers*)   I've never had any need to take shorthand in my position, I said to him. I've a Z.A. in business administration from Philadelphia, and a Z.Z.A. from M.Y.U. night school. I mentioned that I speak a little Spanish of course, and that I'm a whiz at model frigates and warships. (*Steps back.*)

FOURTH INTERVIEWER   Next.

FOURTH APPLICANT (*stepping up to interviewers*)   I can sew a straight seam I said, hand or machine, and I have been exclusively a lady's maid although I *can* cook and will too if I have someone to assist me I said. Unfortunately aside from self-education grammar school is as far as I have progressed. (*Steps back.*)

Each interviewer, during his next speech, bows or curtsies to the applicant nearest him or her.

FIRST INTERVIEWER   Good.

SECOND INTERVIEWER   Fine.

THIRD INTERVIEWER   Very helpful.

FOURTH INTERVIEWER   Thank you.

Each applicant, during his next speech, jumps on the back of the interviewer nearest him or her.

FOURTH APPLICANT   You're welcome, I'm sure.

THIRD APPLICANT   Anything you want to know.

SECOND APPLICANT   Just ask me.

FIRST APPLICANT   Fire away, fire away.

The next eight speeches are spoken simultaneously, with applicants on interviewers' backs.

FIRST INTERVIEWER Well unless there's anything special you want to tell me, I think—

SECOND INTERVIEWER Is there anything more you think I should know about before you—

THIRD INTERVIEWER I wonder if we've left anything out of this questionnaire or if you—

FOURTH INTERVIEWER I suppose I've got all the information down here unless you can—

FIRST APPLICANT I've got kids to support, you know, and I need a job real quick—

SECOND APPLICANT Do you think you could try and get me something today because I—

THIRD APPLICANT How soon you suppose I can expect to hear from your agency? Do you—?

FOURTH APPLICANT I don't like to sound pressureful, but you know I'm currently on unemploy—

Each applicant, during his next speech, jumps off interviewer's back.

FIRST APPLICANT Beggin' your pardon.

SECOND APPLICANT So sorry.

THIRD APPLICANT Excuse me.

FOURTH APPLICANT Go ahead.

Each interviewer, during his next speech, bows and remains in that position.

FIRST INTERVIEWER That's quite all right.

SECOND INTERVIEWER I'm sorry.

THIRD INTERVIEWER I'm sorry.

FOURTH INTERVIEWER My fault.

Each applicant, during his next speech, begins leapfrogging over interviewers' backs.

FIRST APPLICANT My fault.

SECOND APPLICANT My fault.

THIRD APPLICANT I'm sorry.

FOURTH APPLICANT My fault.

Each interviewer, during his next speech, begins leapfrogging too.

FIRST INTERVIEWER That's all right.

SECOND INTERVIEWER My fault.

THIRD INTERVIEWER I'm sorry.

FOURTH INTERVIEWER Excuse *me*.

The leapfrogging continues as the preceding eight lines are repeated simultaneously. Then the interviewers confer in a huddle and come out of it.

FIRST INTERVIEWER Do you enjoy your work?

FIRST APPLICANT Sure, I said, I'm proud. Why not? Sure I know I'm no Rembrandt, I said, but I'm proud of my work, I said to him.

SECOND APPLICANT I told him it stinks. But what am I supposed to do, sit home and rot?

THIRD APPLICANT Do I like my work, he asked me. Well, I said, to gain time, do I like my work? Well, I said, I don't know.

FOURTH APPLICANT I told him right straight out: for a sensible person, a lady's maid is the *only possible* way of life.

SECOND INTERVIEWER Do you think you're irreplaceable?

ALL APPLICANTS Oh, yes indeed.

ALL INTERVIEWERS Irreplaceable?

44

ALL APPLICANTS   Yes, yes indeed.

THIRD INTERVIEWER   Do you like me?

FIRST APPLICANT   You're a nice man.

SECOND APPLICANT   Huh?

THIRD APPLICANT   Why do you ask?

FOURTH APPLICANT   It's not a question of "like."

FIRST INTERVIEWER   Well, we'll be in touch with you.

This is the beginning of leaving the agency. Soft music under. Applicants and interviewers push their seats into two masses of four boxes on either side of the stage. Applicants leave first, joining hands to form a revolving door.

FOURTH INTERVIEWER   What sort of day will it be?

FIRST APPLICANT   I bet we'll have rain.

SECOND APPLICANT   Cloudy, clearing in the afternoon.

THIRD APPLICANT   Mild, I think, with some snow.

FOURTH APPLICANT   Precisely the same as yesterday.

All are now leaving the agency, not in any orderly fashion. Interviewers leave one way and applicants start down the other. The following speeches overlap and are heard indistinctly as crowd noise.

SECOND APPLICANT   Can you get me one?

FIRST INTERVIEWER   See you tomorrow.

THIRD APPLICANT   When will I hear from you?

SECOND INTERVIEWER   We'll let you know.

FOURTH APPLICANT   Where's my umbrella?

THIRD INTERVIEWER   I'm going to a movie.

FIRST INTERVIEWER   So how about it?

FOURTH INTERVIEWER Good night.

THIRD APPLICANT Can you help me, Doctor, I asked.

When all of the actors are offstage, the fourth interviewer makes a siren sound and the following speeches continue as a loud crowd noise for a few moments; they overlap so that the stage is empty only briefly.

FIRST INTERVIEWER It'll take a lot of work on your part.

SECOND INTERVIEWER I'll do what I can for you.

THIRD INTERVIEWER Of course I'll do my best.

FIRST INTERVIEWER God helps those who help themselves.

FIRST APPLICANT I have sinned deeply, Father, I said.

FIRST INTERVIEWER You certainly have. I hope you truly repent.

SECOND INTERVIEWER In the name of the Father, etcetera and the Holy Ghost.

THIRD INTERVIEWER Jesus saves.

FOURTH APPLICANT I said, can you direct me to Fourteenth Street, please?

FIRST INTERVIEWER Just walk down that way a bit and then turn left.

SECOND INTERVIEWER Just walk down that way a bit and then turn right.

THIRD INTERVIEWER Take a cab!

FOURTH APPLICANT Do you hear a siren?

ALL INTERVIEWERS What time is it?

FIRST APPLICANT Half past three.

SECOND APPLICANT It must be about four.

THIRD APPLICANT Half past five.

FOURTH APPLICANT   My watch has stopped.

FIRST INTERVIEWER   Do you enjoy your work?

SECOND INTERVIEWER   Do you think you're irreplaceable?

THIRD INTERVIEWER   Do you like me?

The actor who played the fourth interviewer comes on stage while continuing to make the loud siren noise. The actress who played the fourth applicant comes on stage and speaks directly to the audience.

FOURTH APPLICANT   Can you direct me to Fourteenth Street, please, I said. I seem to have lost my—I started to say, and then I was nearly run down.

The remaining actors return to the stage to play various people on Fourteenth Street—ladies shopping, a panhandler, a man in a sandwich board, a peddler of "franks and orange," a snooty German couple, a lecher, a pair of sighing lovers and so on. Each time the actors approach the audience, they do so as a different character. The actor will need to find the essential vocal and physical mannerisms of each character, play them, and drop them immediately to assume another character. The fourth applicant continues to address the audience directly, to involve them in her hysteria, going up one aisle and back.

I haven't got my social security—I started to say, I saw someone right in front of me and said, could you direct me please to Fourteenth Street, I have to get to Fourteenth Street, please, to get a bargain, I explained, although I could hardly remember what it was I wanted to buy. I read about it in the paper today, I said, only they weren't listening and I said to myself, my purpose for today is to get to—and I couldn't remember, I've set myself the task of—I've got to have—it's that I can save, I remembered I can save if I can get that bargain at—and I couldn't remember where it was so I started to look for my wallet which I seem to have mislaid in my purse, and a man—please watch where you're going, I shouted with my purse half-open, and I seemed to forget—Fourteenth Street, I remembered, and you'd think with all these numbered streets and avenues a person wouldn't get lost—you'd think a person would *help* a person, you'd think so. So I asked the most respectable-looking man I could find, I asked him, please can you direct me to Fourteenth Street. He wouldn't answer. Just wouldn't. I'm lost, I said to myself. The paper said—the television said—they said, I couldn't remember what they said. I turned for help: "Jesus Saves," the sign said, and a man was carrying it, both sides of his body, staring straight ahead. "Jesus Saves," the sign said.

The passersby jostle her more and more.

I couldn't remember where I was going. "Come and be saved," it said, so I asked the man with the sign, please, sir, won't you tell me how to, dear Lord, I thought, anywhere, please, sir, won't you tell me how to—can you direct me to Fourteenth Street, *please!*

The passersby have covered the fourth applicant. All actors mill about until they reach designated positions on the stage where they face the audience, a line of women and a line of men, students in a gym class; the second interviewer has stayed coolly out of the crowd during this last; now he is the gym instructor.

GYM INSTRUCTOR   I took my last drag and strode manfully into the room. Okay, men, I said brightly. Let's see the basic step. *And* breathe it in and two and three and four. And breathe it in and stick it out and three and four. Keep it nice. You want to radiate don't you? You want to radiate that charm and confidence they have in the movies, don't you, I told them. Now ladies. *And* breathe it in and stick 'em out and step right out and four. *And* breathe it in and stick them out. Stick them out. That's what you got them for isn't it? I told them. And keep it nice, all of you. You're selling. Selling all the time. That's right, isn't it, miss? Right, I said. And stick it out and step right out and *smile,* I shouted. And breathe it in and stick it out, step right out and *smile.* Keep it nice. Keep it nice for the other

48

fellow and you'll see how nice it can be for you. *Smile.* Only don't smile so big, I told them. You look like a bunch of creeps when you smile that big, I told them. Smile like you're holding something back, I said, something big, a secret, I said. That's the ticket. Now let's see it. *And* breathe it in and stick it out. Step on out and *smile.* Breathe it in and stick it out. Step on out and *nod.* Step on out and *shake. And* tuck in your butts, I yelled. Step on out and *smile.* Faster, I told them, to see how fast they would go. And breathe it in and stick it out. Step right out and smile. And breathe it in and stick it out. Step right out and smile. And . . .

The rapid movements of the gym class become the vibrations of passengers on a moving subway train. The actors rush to the boxes stage left, continuing to vibrate. Two of the actors stand on the boxes and smile like subway advertisements while the others directly in front of them are pushed against each other on the crowded train. They make an appropriate soft subway noise, a kind of rhythmic hiss, and, as the subway passengers, form their faces into frozen masks of indifference.

SECOND APPLICANT (*squeezing her way to an uncomfortable front seat and speaking half to herself*)   God forgive me . . . you no-good chump, I said to him, I used to love you . . . Not now. Not now . . . God forgive me . . . God forgive me for being old. Not now, I said. I wouldn't wipe the smell off your uncle's bottom now, not for turnips, no. God forgive me . . . Remember how we used to ride the roller coaster out at Coney Island, you and me? Remember? Holding hands in the cold and I'd get so scared and you'd get so scared and we'd hug each other and buy another ticket . . . Remember . . . ? Look now, I said. Look at me, now! God forgive you for leaving me with nothing . . . God forgive you for being dead . . . God forgive me for being alive. . . .

The actress who played the third interviewer slips out of the subway as though it were her stop and sits on a box, stage right, as a telephone operator. The other actors form a telephone circuit by holding hands in two concentric circles around the boxes, stage left; they change the hissing sound of the subway into the whistling of telephone circuits.

TELEPHONE OPERATOR   Just one moment and I will connect you with Information.

The telephone operator alternates her official voice with her ordinary voice; she uses the latter when she talks to her friend Roberta, another operator whom she reaches by flipping a switch. When she is talking to Roberta, the whistling of the telephone circuit changes into a different rhythm and the arms of the actors, which are forming the circuit, move into a different position.

. . . Just one moment and I will connect you with Information. Ow! Listen, Roberta, I said, I've got this terrible cramp. Hang up and dial again please; we find nothing wrong with that number at all. You know what I ate, I said to her, you were there. Baked macaroni, Wednesday special, maplenut fudge, I said. I'm sorry but the number you have reached is not—I can feel it gnawing at me at the bottom of my belly, I told her. Do you think it's serious, Roberta? Appendicitis, I asked. Thank you for giving us the area code but the number you have reached is not in this area. Roberta, I asked her, do you think I have cancer? One moment please, I'm sorry the number you have reached—ow! Well, if it's lunch, Roberta, I said to her, you know what they can do with it tomorrow. Ow! One moment, please, I said. Ow, I said, Roberta, I said, it really hurts.

The telephone operator falls off her seat in pain. The whistling of the telephone circuit becomes a siren. Three actors carry the telephone operator over to the boxes, stage left, which now serve as an operating table. Three actors imitate the telephone operator's breathing pattern while four actors behind her make stylized sounds and movements as surgeons and nurses in the midst of an operation. The telephone operator's breathing accelerates, then stops. After a moment the actors begin spreading over the stage and making the muted sounds of a cocktail party—music, laughter, talk. The actors find a position and remain there, playing various aspects of a party in slow motion and muted tones. They completely ignore the first interviewer, who, as a girl at the party, goes from person to person as if she were in a garden of living statues.

GIRL AT THE PARTY   And then after the ambulance took off I went up in the elevator and into the party. Did you see the accident, I asked, and they said they did, and what did he look like, and I said he wore a brown coat and had straight brown hair. He stepped off the curb right in front of me. We had been walking up the same block, he a few feet ahead of me, this block right here, I said, but she wasn't listening. Hi, my name is Jill, I said to somebody sitting down and they looked at me and smiled so I said his arm was torn out of its socket and his face was on the pavement gasping but I didn't touch him and she smiled and walked away and I said after her, you aren't supposed to touch someone before—I *wanted* to help, I said, but she wasn't listening. When a man came up and said, was it someone you knew and I said, yes, it was someone I knew slightly, someone I knew, yes, and he offered me a drink and I said no thanks, I didn't want one, and he said well how well did I know him, and I said I knew him well, yes, I knew him very well. You were coming together to the party, he said. Yes, I said, excuse me. Hi, my name is Jill, did you hear a siren, and they said, oh you're the one who saw it, was he killed? (*She has been speaking rapidly and excitedly, but now she begins to be resigned to the fact that no one is listening.*) And I said, yes I was, excuse me, and went back across the room but couldn't find another face to talk to until I deliberately bumped into somebody because I had to tell them one of us couldn't come because of the accident. It was Jill. Jill couldn't come. I'm awfully sorry, I said, because of the accident. She had straight brown hair, I said, and was wearing a brown coat, and two or three people looked at me strangely and moved off. I'm sorry I said to a man, and I laughed, and moved off. I'm dead I said to several people and started to push them over, I'm dead, thank you, I said, thank you, please, I said, I'm dead, until two or three of them got hold of my arms and hustled me out.

I'm sorry, I said, I couldn't come because of the accident. I'm sorry. Excuse me.

The girl at the party is lowered to the floor by two of the men and then all fall down except the actor who played the fourth interviewer. He remains seated as a psychiatrist. The third applicant, on the floor, props his head up on his elbow and speaks to the audience.

THIRD APPLICANT   Can you help me, Doctor, I asked him.

The psychiatrist crosses his legs and assumes a professional expression.

THIRD APPLICANT   Well, it started, well it started, I said, when I was sitting in front of the television set with my feet on the coffee table. Now I've sat there hundreds of times, thousands maybe, with a can of beer in my hand. I like to have a can of beer in my hand when I watch the beer ads. But now for no reason I can think of, the ad was making me sick. So I used the remote control to get to another channel, but each channel made me just as sick. The television was one thing and I was a person, and I was going to be sick. So I turned it off and had a panicky moment. I smelled the beer in my hand and as I vomited I looked around the living room for something to grab on to, something to look at, but there was just our new furniture. I tried to get ahold of myself. I tried to stare straight ahead above the television set, at a little spot on the wall I know. I've had little moments like that before, Doctor, I said, panicky little moments like that when the earth seems to slip out from under, and everything whirls around and you try to hold on to something, some object, some thought, but I couldn't think of anything. Later the panic went away, I told him, it went away, and I'm much better now. But I don't feel like doing anything anymore, except sit and stare at the wall. I've lost my job. Katherine thought I should come and see you. Can you help me, Doctor, I asked him.

PSYCHIATRIST
Blah, blah, blah, blah, blah, blah, *hostile.*
Blah, blah, blah, blah, blah, blah, *penis.*

Blah, blah, blah, blah, blah, blah, *mother*. (*holding out his hand*)
Blah, blah, blah, blah, blah, blah, *money*.

*The third applicant takes the psychiartrist's hand and gets up, extending
his left hand to the next actor. This begins a grand right and left with all
the actors all over the stage.*

ALL (*chanting as they do the grand right and left*)

Blah, blah, blah, blah, blah, blah, *hostile*.
Blah, blah, blah, blah, blah, blah, *penis*.
Blah, blah, blah, blah, blah, blah, *mother*.
Blah, blah, blah, blah, blah, blah, *money*.
Blah, blah, blah, blah, blah, blah, *hostile*.
Blah, blah, blah, blah, blah, blah, *penis*.
Blah, blah, blah, blah, blah, blah, *mother*.
Blah, blah, blah, blah, blah, blah, *money*.

*They form couples and lock hands with arms crossed, continuing to moue,
but in a smaller circle.*

Blah, blah, blah, blah, blah, blah, blah.
Blah, blah, blah, blah, blah, blah, blah.

*Now they slow down to the speed of a church procession. The women bow
their heads, letting their hair fall forward over their faces. The "blah, blah,
blah" continues, but much more slowly while some of the women
accompany it with a descant of* Kyrie Eleison. *After they have gone
around in a circle once this way, the actor who played the fourth interviewer
sits with his back to the audience as a priest. The first applicant kneels next
to him, facing the audience as if in a confessional booth. The other six actors
are at the back of the stage in two lines, swaying slightly, heads down. The
women are in front with their hair still down over their faces.*

FIRST APPLICANT (*crossing himself perfunctorily and starting to speak;
his manner is not impassioned; it is clear that he comes regularly to
repeat this always fruitless ritual*)   Can you help me, Father, I
said, as I usually do, and he said, as usual, nothing. I'm your

friend, the housepainter, I said, the good housepainter. Remember me, Father? He continued as usual to say nothing. Almost the only color you get to paint these days, Father, I said, is white. Only white, Father, I said not expecting any more from him than usual, but going on anyway. The color I really like to paint, Father, is red, I said. Pure brick red. Now there's a confession, Father. He said nothing. I'd like to take a trip to the country, Father, I said, and paint a barn door red, thinking that would get a rise out of him, but it didn't. God, I said then, deliberately taking the Lord's name in vain, the result of taking a three-inch brush and lightly kissing a coat of red paint on a barn door is something stunning and beautiful to behold. He still said nothing. Father, I said, springing it on him, Father, I'd like to join a monastery. My wife's sister, she could take care of the kids. Still nothing. Father, I said again, I'd like to join a monastery. Can you help me, Father? Nothing. Father, I said, I've tried lots of things in my life, I've gone in a lot of different directions, Father, and none of them seems any better than any other, Father, I said. Can you help me, Father, I said. But he said nothing as usual, and then, as usual, I went away.

The first applicant and the fourth interviewer, who hasn't moved at all during the confession, move upstage to join the others as the music starts up violently in a rock beat. The actors do a rock version of the Virginia reel.

SECOND INTERVIEWER (*loudly*)   My

All bow to partners.

FOURTH APPLICANT (*loudly*)   fault.

All do-si-do

SECOND APPLICANT (*loudly*)   Excuse

All circle around.

FOURTH INTERVIEWER (*loudly*)   me.

All peel off.

FIRST INTERVIEWER (*loudly*)   Can you

SECOND APPLICANT (*loudly*)   help

FIRST APPLICANT (*loudly*)   me?

FOURTH INTERVIEWER (*loudly*)   Next.

All continue dancing, joining hands at the center to form a revolving door again. They repeat the preceding eight speeches. Then the second interviewer speaks rapidly as a square dance caller.

SECOND INTERVIEWER   Step right up, ladies and gents, and shake the hand of the next governor of this state. Shake his hand and say hello. Tell your friends you shook the hand of the next governor of the state. Step right up and shake his hand. Ask him questions. Tell him problems. Say hello. Step right up, shake his hand, shake the hand, ladies and gents, of the next governor of the state. Tell your folks: I shook his hand. When he's famous you'll be proud. Step right up, ladies and gents, and shake his hand. Ask him questions. Tell him problems. Say hello. Step right up, ladies and gents. Don't be shy. Shake the hand of the next governor of this state.

The actors have formed a crowd, downstage right, facing the audience. They give the impression of being but a few of a great number of people, all trying to squeeze to the front to see and speak to the political candidate. The fourth interviewer, now playing a politician, stands on a box, stage left, facing the audience. The second interviewer stands by the crowd and keeps it in order.

POLITICIAN   Thank you very much, I said cheerfully, and good luck to you, I said, turning my smile to the next one.

The first interviewer, panting as the girl at the party, squeezes out of the crowd and rushes up to the politician, who smiles at her benignly.

POLITICIAN   Our children *are* our most important asset, I agreed earnestly. Yes they are, I said solemnly. Children, I said, with a long pause, are our most important asset. I only wish I could, madame, I said earnestly, standing tall, but rats, I said regretfully, are a city matter.

The first interviewer returns to the crowd while the third interviewer, as the telephone operator, rushes up to the politician. She appeals to him, making the same noise she made when her stomach hurt her.

POLITICIAN   Nobody knows more about red tape than I do, I said knowingly, and I wish you luck, I said, turning my smile to the next one.

The third interviewer returns to the crowd and the fourth applicant goes up to the politician.

POLITICIAN   I certainly will, I said, with my eyes sparkling, taking a pencil out of my pocket. And what's your name, I said, looking at her sweetly and signing my name at the same time. That's a lovely name, I said.

The fourth applicant returns to the crowd while the third applicant, as an older man, shakes the politician's hand.

POLITICIAN   Yes sir, I said, those were the days. And good luck to you, sir, I said respectfully but heartily, and look out for the curb, I said, turning my smile to the next one.

The third applicant returns to the crowd and the second applicant approaches the politician.

POLITICIAN   Indeed yes, the air we breathe *is* foul, I said indignantly. I agree with you entirely, I said wholeheartedly. And if my opponent wins it's going to get worse, I said with conviction. We'd all die within ten years, I said. And good luck to you, madame, I said politely, and turned my smile to the next one.

The first applicant approaches him, his cap in his hand.

POLITICIAN Well, I said confidingly, getting a bill through the legislature is easier said than done, but answering violence, I said warningly, with violence, I said earnestly, is not the answer, and how do you do I said, turning my smile to the next one.

Next two sighing lovers, whom we saw on Fourteenth Street played by the first and second interviewers, approach the politician.

POLITICIAN No, I said, I never said my opponent would kill us all. No, I said, I never said that. May the best man win, I said manfully.

Halfhearted cheers. The first and second interviewer return to the crowd.

POLITICIAN Do you want us shaking hands, I asked the photographer, turning my profile to the left. Good-bye, I said cheerfully, and good luck to you too. I do feel, I said without false modesty, that I'm better qualified in the field of foreign affairs than my opponents are, yes, I said, *but,* I said, with a pause for emphasis, foreign policy is the business of the President, not the governor, therefore I will say nothing about the war, I said with finality.

The crowd makes a restive sound, then freezes.

I'm sorry, I said seriously, but I'll have to study the question a good deal more before I can answer it.

The crowd makes a louder protest, then freezes.

Of course, I said frowning, one thing is certain, we must all support the President, I said as I turned concernedly to the next one.

Crowd makes a very angry sound, then freezes.

I'm sorry about the war, I said. Nobody sorrier than I am, I said sorrowfully. But I'm afraid, I said gravely, that there are no easy answers. (*Smiles, pleased with himself.*) Good luck to you too, I said cheerfully, and turned my smile to the next one.

The politician topples from his box, beginning his speech all over again. Simultaneously, all the other characters lurch about the stage, speaking again in character—the shopper on Fourteenth Street, the gym instructor, the subway rider, the telephone operator, the girl at the party, the analysand and the house painter. Simultaneously they all stop and freeze, continue again, freeze again, then continue with music under. The second interviewer, acting as policeman, begins to line them up in a diagonal line, like marching dolls, one behind the other. As they are put into line they begin to move their mouths without sound, like fish in a tank. The music stops. When all are in line the second interviewer joins them.

SECOND INTERVIEWER My

FOURTH APPLICANT fault.

SECOND APPLICANT Excuse

FOURTH INTERVIEWER me.

FIRST INTERVIEWER Can you

SECOND APPLICANT help

FIRST APPLICANT me?

FOURTH INTERVIEWER Next.

All continue marching in line, moving their mouths and shouting their lines as the lights come slowly down.

SECOND INTERVIEWER My

FOURTH APPLICANT fault.

SECOND APPLICANT Excuse

FOURTH INTERVIEWER me.

FIRST INTERVIEWER Can you

SECOND APPLICANT help

FIRST APPLICANT me?

FOURTH INTERVIEWER Next.

CURTAIN

TV

photo by Phill Niblock

TV was first presented as part of *America Hurrah* at the Pocket Theatre, New York City.

TV

The youth Narcissus mistook his own reflection in the water for another person . . . He was numb. He had adapted to his extension of himself and had become a closed system.

MARSHALL McLUHAN

The set is white and impersonal. There are two doors on the stage right wall: one leads to the rest rooms, the other to the hall.

Downstage right is the control console in a television viewing room. It faces the audience.

Above the console, also facing the audience, is a screen. Projected on it, from the rear, is the logo of a television station.

Downstage left is a water cooler, a closet for coats and a telephone. Downstage right is a bulletin board. Upstage center is a table with a coffeemaker on it.

Hal and Susan are seated at the console. Susan sits in the middle chair. They are both in their twenties. Hal is playing, as he often will, with his penknife: whittling pencils, paring his nails or throwing the knife at the bulletin board. Susan is involved with the papers on the console, with sharpening pencils and so forth.

At the back of the stage, on the left, are the five actors who will portray what will appear on television. For the moment they have no light on them and their backs are to the audience.

To indicate the correlation of the events and dialogue on television with those which occur in the viewing room, the play is printed in two columns.

HAL So what do you say?

SUSAN I don't know.

HAL That doesn't get us very far, does it?

SUSAN Well it's such a surprise, your asking. I was planning to work on my apartment.

HAL I'll help you, after the movie.

SUSAN That's too late. One thing I have to have is eight hours' sleep. I really have to have that.

George enters; he is older than Hal and Susan, and is in charge of the viewing room.

HAL Hi, George.

SUSAN Hello, George.

GEORGE (*to Susan*) Is that a new dress?

SUSAN (*nodding toward Hal*) *He* didn't even notice.

George puts his coat and jacket in the closet and puts on a cardigan sweater.

GEORGE How many check marks have you made, Hal?

HAL I don't know, George. I don't count.

SUSAN I got it on Fourteenth Street. I love going into places like that because they're so cheap.

GEORGE If you don't make at least a hundred check marks, they'll dock you. That's what the totals count column is for.

SUSAN (*looking at herself in a mirror*) Have I lost any weight?

GEORGE Where would you lose it from?

HAL George, how come they haven't asked us for a detailed report in nearly three weeks?

GEORGE How should I know?

HAL Think they're forgetting about us, George?

SUSAN I was trying to tell in the Ladies, but the fluorescent light in there just burns your eyes.

HAL I've never been to the Ladies. You think I'd like it?

GEORGE This viewing room is the backbone of the rating system.

HAL He said that to you *last* month, George. Things move fast.

GEORGE Are you trying to make me nervous?

HAL Maybe.

GEORGE Well don't, because my stomach is not very good this morning.

SUSAN I want to know seriously, and I mean seriously, do you think I've lost any weight?

GEORGE Where from?

HAL Why don't you let yourself go?

SUSAN What do you mean?

HAL Just let nature take its course.

SUSAN What if nature wants you to be a big fat slob?

HAL Then be a big fat slob.

SUSAN Thanks.

Hal, Susan and George sit down and get ready for the day's work. George turns a dial on the console which turns on the TV. Two of the people on television turn around to play Helen and Harry Fargis.

All of the people on television are dressed in shades of gray. They make no costume changes and use no real props. Their faces are made up with thin horizontal black lines to suggest the way they might appear to a viewer. They are playing television images. Their style of action is cool, not pushy. As television characters, they have only a few facial masks, such as "cute," "charming" or "serious" which they use infallibly, like signals, in the course of each television segment. After each television segment, the people involved in it will freeze where they are until it is time for them to become another character.

As the play progresses, the people on television will use more and more of the stage. The impression should be that of a slow invasion of the viewing room. Hal, Susan and George will simply move around the people on television when that becomes necessary. Ultimately, the control console itself will be taken over by television characters, so that the distinction between what is on television and what is occurring in the viewing room will be lost completely.

The attention of the audience should be focused not on a parody of television, but on the relationship of the life that appears on television to the life that goes on in the viewing room. All of the actors will need to be constantly aware of what is happening on all parts of the stage, in order to give and take the attention of the audience to and from each other, and also in order to demonstrate the influence of the style of certain television segments on the behavior of Hal, Susan and George.

HAL   Why try to look like somebody else ?

Helen and Harry Fargis are at home. Helen is baking cookies.

HELEN   Harry, what are you working on in the garage?

SUSAN   I'm trying to look like myself thin. Very thin.

HARRY   If I succeed in my experiments, nobody in the world will be hungry for love. Ever again.

HAL (*offering him one*)   Want a cigarette, George?

GEORGE   No, thanks.

HELEN   Hungry for love? Harry, you make me nervous.

67

HAL Just one?

GEORGE No.

SUSAN Hal, why don't you try to help George instead of being so cruel.

HAL I'm just offering him a cigarette.

GEORGE (*as Hal takes the cigarette away*) Give me one.

SUSAN Hal, that's utter torture for George.

GEORGE Give me one.

HELEN You really do.

HARRY Men will put down their arms.

HELEN You haven't been to work for a week now. You'll lose your job.

HARRY You don't understand. This is more important.

HELEN Oh, Harry. I don't understand you at all anymore. I really don't.

Harry goes back to the garage. Helen mumbles to herself as she cleans up the kitchen.

HELEN I don't know.

HELEN I just don't know. He used to be so docile.

SUSAN Don't, George. He's just playing cat and mouse.

HELEN And now I just don't know—

HARRY (*calling from garage*) Helen!

HELEN Harry?

HAL That's right, George. Don't have one. I'm just playing cat and mouse. (*He lights a cigarette.*)

HARRY Helen, my experiments.

HELEN Harry, what?

GEORGE Just give it to me, will you?

HARRY A terrible mistake.

SUSAN Try to control yourself for just another half hour, George.

HELEN Harry, your voice . . !

GEORGE No.

SUSAN Why not?

HARRY (*this voice getting lower and gruffer*) For the love of heaven, Helen, keep away from me.

HELEN What happened?

GEORGE Because I don't wanna control myself for just another half hour.

HAL Whatever you want, George. (*hands a cigarette to George*)

HARRY I can't restrain myself anymore. I'm coming through the garage door. (*He comes through the garage door, wearing a monster mask; his voice is now very deep and gruff.*) I'm irresistibly attracted to you, Helen, irresistibly.

HELEN Eeeeeeeeeeeeeeeee eeceeeeeeeek!

HARRY (*stepping toward her*) Helen, I love you. (*goes to embrace her*)

HELEN Harry, you're hideous. Eeeeek! Eeeeeeeeeeeeeek! Eeeeeceeeeeek!

As Helen screams, Wonderboy is discovered in mufti, doing his homework.

SUSAN What was the point of that, Hal?

HAL No point.

WONDERBOY Two super-quantums plus five uranium neutrons, and I've got the minisub fuel. Hooray. Boy, will my friends in the U.S. Navy be pleased. Hey, what's that? Better use my wonder-vision. Helen Fargis seems to be in trouble. Better change to Wonderboy (*as if throwing open his shirt*) and fly over there in a flash (*jumping as if flying*). I guess I'm in the nick of time. (*With one superpowerful punch in the jaw he subdues Harry, the monster.*)

HELEN Oh, Wonderboy, what would have happened if you hadn't come? But what will happen to *It*?

WONDERBOY I'll fly him to a distant zoo where they'll take good care of him.

HELEN Oh, Wonderboy, how can I ever repay you?

WONDERBOY Are those home-baked cookies I smell?

SUSAN The president of the company has an Eames chair.

Helen smiles at Wonderboy through her tears; he puts his arm around her shoulders.

WONDERBOY Tune in tomorrow, boys and girls, when I'll subdue a whole countryful of monsters.

GEORGE How do you know that?

WONDERBOY And in the meantime, remember: winners eat Wondrex.

71

SUSAN Jennifer showed it to me.

GEORGE You asked to see it?

SUSAN Don't worry, George. He wasn't there. I just had this crazy wild impulse as I was passing his office. I wanted to see what it looked like. Isn't that wild?

HAL Did you sit in it?

SUSAN I didn't dare. What would I have said if he'd come in?

George goes to the rest room.

HAL I love you, Mr. President of my great big company, and that's why I'm sitting in your nice warm leather armchair.

SUSAN You're perverted. I don't want to be a person working in a company who's never seen her president.

Smiles and jumps in the air, as if flying away.

FIRST NEWS ANNOUNCER
Little girls with big shopping bags means back-to-school season is here again. Among the many shoppers in downtown New York were Darlene, nine, Lila, four, and Lucy Gladden, seven, of Lynbrook, Long Island.

FIRST NEWS ANNOUNCER In Washington, D.C., as he left John Foster Dulles Airport, as the President's favorite

FIRST NEWS ANNOUNCER
representative, the Vice President said he was bursting with confidence.

U. S. spokesmen in Saigon
said families would be given
adequate shelter and
compensation. Our planes
are under strict orders not
to return to base with any
bombs. The United States
regrets that a friendly village
was hit. The native toll was
estimated at sixty.

SUSAN (*to Hal, who has
gotten up*) While you're
up—

HAL What?

SUSAN You know. Get me a
Coke. (*titters at her own
joke*)

*Hal goes out through hall door.
George returns from the rest room.*

SECOND NEWS ANNOUNCER
This was high, explained
spokesmen, in answer to
questions, because of the
type of bomb dropped. These
are known as Lazy Dogs.
Each Lazy Dog bomb
contains ten thousand slivers
of razor-sharp steel.

GEORGE (*turning TV sound
off*) Can I come over
tonight?

SUSAN Not tonight. (*goes to
bulletin board*)

*Two people on television do a
silent commercial for Longford*

73

cigarettes: a man lights a woman's cigarette and she looks pleased.

GEORGE (*following her*)   Why not tonight?

SUSAN   Because I don't feel like it.

GEORGE   You have a date?

SUSAN   What business is that of yours? Don't think because—

GEORGE   Who with?

SUSAN   None of your business.

GEORGE   What about late, after you get back, like one o'clock.

SUSAN   That's too late. I need lots of sleep.

GEORGE   I'll call first.

SUSAN   You'd better.

Whenever Hal, Susan and George have nothing else to do, they stare straight ahead, as if at a television screen. George and Susan do this now. Hal comes back with two Cokes.

George goes to the telephone and dials it.

GEORGE   Hello, dear. Yes, I'm here. Listen, I'm afraid I have to take the midnight-to-three shift.

Sally and Bill are two characters in a Western.

74

SALLY Don't go, Bill.

BILL I've got to.

GEORGE I've got to. The night supervisor is out.

SALLY Oh, Bill.

GEORGE And I've already said I would.

Bill leaves.

SALLY Oh, Bill.

GEORGE Listen, let's talk about it over dinner, huh? I'll be out after you go to sleep and in before you wake up so what's the difference? Listen, let's talk about it over dinner I said. Listen, I love you. Good-bye. (*Hangs up.*)

Sally fixes her hair in the mirror.

HAL (*watching TV intently, but talking to George*) You have to take the rnidnight-to-three shift, George? That's really too bad.

She is surprised by Steve, the villian, who has just been waiting for Bill to ride off.

SALLY Steve!

HAL Got a call while I was out?

STEVE Bill's dead, Sally.

SALLY I don't believe you.

GEORGE (*snapping the sound out on the Western*) Do either of you want to take

Steve tries to embrace Sally. She slaps him

on some evening overtime
this week?

SUSAN Which?

hard as he approaches her.
He tries it again. She slaps
him again. He tries
it a third time. She gets him
a third time. Then he grabs
and kisses her despite her
terrible struggling.

GEORGE Five to midnight
Tuesday and Thursday.

HAL Thursday.

SUSAN Oh, all right, I'll take
Tuesday.

HAL Did you want Thursday?

SUSAN I'd like to get the
apartment finished.

HAL Then give me Tuesday.

SUSAN Not if you *have*
something on Thursday.

HAL No sweat.

SUSAN Oh, *I* know. It was
That talk with that man.

Bill, his arm wounded,
appears again. Seeing
Steve with Sally, he
draws and aims.

BILL Sally, duck!

GEORGE What talk with
what man?

SUSAN A man he has to
talk to.

GEORGE About a job?

Sally ducks. Bill
shoots Steve, then goes to
Sally to make sure she's
all right. Steve, how-

76

HAL I probably won't even see him.

GEORGE What kind of job?

HAL For the government. I tell you I probably won't see him.

GEORGE If you quit, Hal, I'll need three weeks' notice. If you care about severance pay.

HAL I haven't seen him yet, even.

GEORGE Or about me.

HAL I wasn't going to mention it.

SUSAN I'm sorry. It was my fault.

GEORGE Just don't spring anything on me. If you don't like the job, leave. But don't spring anything on me because I can't take it, you know that.

ever, it not badly wounded and he reaches for Bill's gun. The gun falls to the floor and they fight. Sally tries to get into the fight but is pushed away.

Bill is losing his fight with Steve because of his wounded arm. Steve is about to get the gun.

SALLY (*warningly*) Bill!

In the nick of time, Sally shoots Steve in the back with a rifle. As he falls he makes a mute appeal to her. He is dead now and she is appalled at what she's done.

HAL   George, I'm *not* quitting.

SUSAN   He likes this job too much, George.

HAL   I love it more than my own life. I wouldn't leave it for all the world. Honest Injun, George.

GEORGE   Can you imagine what I'd have to go through to train another person? Can you?

SALLY (*embracing Bill*)   Oh, Bill!

BILL   I love you, Sally.

SALLY (*touched*)   Oh, Bill.

BILL   Let's move to another town.

SALLY (*delighted*)   Oh, Bill.

Bill and Sally ride off together into the dusk.

SUSAN   Listen, I just remembered a joke. There's this writing on the subway. "I love grills," it says on the wall. So somebody crosses out "grills" and writes in "girls." "I love girls," it says now. And then somebody else writes in, "What about us grills?" (*She laughs and laughs over this.*)

Hal turns on volume.

SUSAN   What about us grills? Isn't that fantastic?

The President is accompanied by his wife, and by his two daughters, who live in nearby Austin with their husbands, the President's sons-in-law.

HAL   What's the matter with you?

The President appears at a podium reading a speech. He is indeed accompanied by his wife and daughters.

SUSAN *(still laughing)*   I think that's the funniest thing I ever heard.

HAL   Shhhh.

PRESIDENT   We will stamp out aggression wherever and whenever . . .

Susan continues laughing.

HAL   Shhhhh. Stop it.

SUSAN   I can't.

SUSAN   I can't stop. Get the water.

PRESIDENT   We will tighten our defenses and fight, to guarantee the peace of our children, our childen's children and their children.

George gets up to get some water. Hal wants to watch the television and can't hear it at all because of Susan's laughter.

PRESIDENT   That all men are not well-intentioned or well-

79

informed or even basically good is unfortunate.

HAL This is easier. (*He slaps Susan very hard on the face.*)

SUSAN Ow!

PRESIDENT But these people will not be indulged.

SUSAN Just who do you think you are!

Applause by the President's family. No sound in this play need be put on tape; all of it can be provided by the people on television.

HAL Are you finished?

SUSAN I couldn't help it.

PRESIDENT Those who are our friends will declare themselves publicly. The others, we will not tolerate.

SUSAN Sadist.

PRESIDENT Belief in American success and victory is the cornerstone of our faith.

SUSAN Why didn't anyone get water?

GEORGE Don't look at me.

PRESIDENT Whatever else may chance to happen on far-off shores, nothing—I repeat, nothing—will be allowed to disturb the peace and serenity of our cities and suburbs, and when we fight we fight for a safer and more comfortable America, now and in years to come. Thank you.

SUSAN   You don't slap people because they're sick.

HAL   Every day we go through the same thing. You laugh. We bring you water. You spill the water all over everybody, and half an hour later you stop.

SECOND NEWS ANNOUNCER
The President and his family will now be cheered by the cheered by the cadet corps.

SUSAN   Give me the water, George. I'm going to take a pill.

The President and his family respond to cheers like mechanical dolls. Turning his back, the second news announcer provides us with one hummed bar of "Hello, Dolly."

GEORGE   What makes you laugh like that?

A Spanish teacher appears.

Hal lowers the volume but does not turn it off.

SUSAN   I'm a hysteric. I mean I'm not constantly hysterical but sometimes I get that way. I react that way, through my body. You're a compulsive, Hal, a nasty little compulsive.

SPANISH TEACHER   *Buenos dias, muchachos* and *muchachas.* Hello, boys and girls. *Muchachos.* Boys. *Muchachas.* Girls. *Aquí está la casa.* Here is the house. *Casa.* House.

81

HAL How do you know?

SUSAN I've discussed it with my analyst. Hysterics react through their bodies. Compulsives react compulsively.

GEORGE What does he say about me?

SUSAN He doesn't.

GEORGE Humph.

HAL How long have you been going now? Twenty-seven years?

SUSAN A year, wise guy.

HAL How long do you expect to be going?

SUSAN It might take another two or three years.

GEORGE I know people who have gone for ten or twelve years.

HAL Don't you think that's a lot?

GEORGE If you need it, you need it. It's a sickness like any other sickness. It's got to be looked after.

HAL What did they do in the old days?

Efficient reseachers walk back and forth across the stage, checking things, nodding at each other curtly, and so on.

82

GEORGE   They stayed sick.

UGP ANNOUNCER   Who are they? They are a community of devotion.

UGP ANNOUNCER   Men and women whose lives are dedicated to the researching of more perfect products for you. Get the benefit of a community of devotion. Look for the letters UGP whenever you buy a car, radio, television set or any of a thousand other products. Their tool: devotion. Their goal: perfection.

SUSAN   My analyst has been going to *his* analyst for twenty-five years.

HAL   How do you know?

SUSAN   He told me.

FIRST NEWS ANNOUNCER   Three men were critically injured during a civil rights demonstration in Montgomery, Alabama today.

GEORGE   Can you feel the tranquilizer working?

SUSAN   A little bit. I think so.

FIRST NEWS ANNOUNCER This afternoon the Vice President arrived in Honolulu. As he stepped off the plane he told newsmen things are looking up.

GEORGE Maybe I should have one too.

FIRST NEWS ANNOUNCER The Defense Department today conceded that United States aircraft may have mistakenly flown over Chinese territory last month. If this is so, said a spokesman, we're sorry.

SUSAN (*turning volume off*) Are you upset?

GEORGE I can feel my stomach. *A rock-and-roll group is seen singing and playing.*

SUSAN (*reaching into her bag to give him a pill*) Here.

GEORGE I'd like some coffee.

HAL I'd like some lunch.

SUSAN Lunch! I'll get it. (*dashes into her coat and is almost out the door*)

HAL Hey!

SUSAN Rare with onion and a danish. I know. So long, you guys.

HAL (*throwing his penknife into the bulletin board*) Think she's all right?

GEORGE People wouldn't say this was a crazy office or anything like that.

HAL Nope.

GEORGE She's really a nice girl, isn't she?

HAL (*doing calisthenics*) Yup.

GEORGE You like her, don't you?

HAL Yup.

GEORGE I mean you don't just think she's a good lay, do you?

HAL What makes you think I lay her?

GEORGE Well, don't you?

HAL George, that's an old trick.

GEORGE I'm just trying to find out if you really like her.

HAL Why do you care?

GEORGE I feel protective.

HAL That's right. She's half your age, isn't she?

GEORGE Not exactly half.

HAL How old are you, George, exactly?

GEORGE Forty-three.

HAL (*crossing to water cooler*) Humph.

GEORGE What's that mean?

HAL I was just wondering what it was like to be forty-three.

GEORGE It stinks.

HAL That's what I thought.

GEORGE You'll be forty-three sooner than you think.

HAL I'll never be forty-three.

GEORGE Why not?

HAL I don't intend to live that long.

The rock-and-roll group bows.

GEORGE You have something?

HAL No. I just don't intend to that live that long. (*He returns to the console and turns the volume on.*)

A group of peace marchers appears.

FIRST NEWS ANNOUNCER A group of so-called peaceniks marched down the center mall of the capital today, singing:

GEORGE (*sits*) You're probably a Socialist.

The peace marchers sing "We Shall Overcome."

86

HAL   A Socialist?

GEORGE   A Socialist at twenty and
a Republican at forty.
Everybody goes through that
cycle.

FIRST NEWS ANNOUNCER   One
young man from New York
City predicted:

**ONE YOUNG MAN FROM NEW
YORK CITY**   The Washington Monument's going to
burst into bloom and—

*It is as if the sound were cut off
on the word he was going to
say, our we can read "Fuck"
on his lips.*

GEORGE   It's healthy.

FIRST NEWS ANNOUNCER   A
little girl, Annie Kappelhoff,
had her own opinion:

ANNIE   (*as if leading a
cheer*)   Burn yourselves, not
your draft cards, burn yourselves, not your draftcards—

*The sound is cut off on Annie,
too, as she continues the same
cheer.*

FIRST NEWS ANNOUNCER   Later
in the day Annie was the star
of her own parade. She's
head cheerleader of Wilumet
High School in Maryland.
Today Annie cheered her

87

team on to victory, thirty to nothing, over neighboring South Dearing. Annie is also an ardent supporter of the Young American Nazi party, and hopes to become a model. And now, a message.

HAL   Are you a Republican, George?

FAMOUS TV PERSONALITY   Are you one of those lucky women who has all the time in the world?

GEORGE   That's right.

HAL   You know I have a lot of friends who won't even speak to Republicans.

GEORGE   I'd rather not discuss politics.

FAMOUS TV PERSONALITY   Or are you like most of us: busy, busy, busy all day long with home or job so that when evening comes you hardly have time to wash your face face, much less transform yourself into the living doll he loves.

HAL   Why not?

GEORGE   Because we probably don't see eye to eye.

HAL   So?

GEORGE   So I'd rather not discuss it. And my stomach's upset.

FAMOUS TV PERSONALITY   Well then, K-F is for you. More than a soap. More than a cream. It's a soap-cream. You apply it in less time than it takes to wash your face and it leaves your skin tingling with loveliness. Try it. And for an extra super thrill, use it in the shower.

LILY HEAVEN'S ANNOUNCER
The Lily Heaven Show, ladies and gentlemen, starring that great star of stage, screen and television: Lily Heaven.

Out through imaginary curtains comes Lily Heaven, very starlike. She greets her audience in her own inimitable way and sings a few lines of a popular American love song.

There is a special knock on the viewing room door.

HAL What's that?

GEORGE Nothing.

George turns volume off.

HAL What do you mean, nothing?

GEORGE (*calling*) One minute.

HAL (*getting panicky*) One minute until what?

George turns out the lights in the viewing room.

HAL I knew it. What's going on?

GEORGE (*calling*) Okay.

HAL Okay what? What? What?

SUSAN (*coming through the door with a cake with lighted candles on it*) Okay this, stupid.

HAL Oh my God, you're crazy.

SUSAN AND GEORGE One, two, three. (*singing*)

Happy birthday to you,
Happy birthday to you,
Happy birthday dear Ha-al,
Happy birthday to you.

Susan turns volume off. She kisses Hal on the lips.

SUSAN Happy birthday. You had no idea, did you?

HAL No.

GEORGE Happy birthday.

HAL Thanks a lot.

SUSAN Make a wish and blow.

Hal blows on the candles but doesn't get them all. George turns the viewing-room lights on again and Susan gets two presents from the closet.

SUSAN Well, almost. People thought I was crazy walking down the hall with this cake and this lunch in a paper bag. And I was petrified one of you would swing the door open while I was waiting in

the corridor and knock me
down and the cake and
everything. I was almost sure
you'd guessed, Hal, when I
put the presents in my locker
this morning.

HAL   I hadn't.

SUSAN   I love birthdays. I know
it's childish but I really do.
Look at the card on George's.

HAL   It's cute.

SUSAN   Open it.

Hal opens the package. It's a tie.

HAL   Well, thanks, George. I
can use this. *He makes a mock
noose of it around his neck.*

GEORGE   You're welcome.

SUSAN (*looking at the label as if she
hadn't seen it before*)   It's a
good tie.

GEORGE   What'd you expect?

*George is biting into an egg salad
sandwich. Hal starts to open the
second present.*

SUSAN (*stopping Hal*)   Save mine
for when we eat the cake, so
the birthday will last longer.

HAL   George, there's egg salad
all over the dials.

GEORGE (*turning up volume*)
Sorry.

SUSAN Here's a napkin. I'll make
some coffee.

GEORGE Good.

LILY HEAVEN So long,
everybody.

LILY HEAVEN This is Lily
Heaven saying so long.

*Part of Lily Heaven's
audience, played by the people
on television who stand
behind her, applauds.*

LILY HEAVEN (*as if each sentence
were her last*) Here's wishing
you a good week before we
meet again. From all of us
here to all of you out there:
so long. Thanks a lot and
God bless you. This is Lily
signing off. I only hope that
you enjoyed watching us as
much as we enjoyed being
here. So long. It's been
wonderful being with you.
Really grand, and I hope
you'll invite us into your
living room again next
week. I only wish we could
go on but I'm afraid it's time
to say so long, so from the
actors and myself, from the
staff here, I want to wish you
all a very very good week.

92

George and Hal are mesmerized by Lily Heaven. Susan is paying no attention but is fussing with the coffee things and putting paper bags, as party hats, on Hal and George.

GEORGE Give me another of those tranquilizers, please. The first one doesn't seem to have done a thing.

Hal turns the volume off. Susan has plugged in the hot plate and coffeemaker. She also has some real coffee and a jar of dried cream, some sugar and sugar substitutes in little bags stolen from a luncheonette, napkins and little wooden stick-stirrers.

HAL (*who has been opening his present*) Say, this is nice.

SUSAN It's an art book.

HAL I can see that.

GEORGE Hal especially interested in art?

SUSAN A person doesn't have to be especially interested in art to like it.

HAL It must have cost a lot, Susan. Here, George. (*passes George a piece of cake*)

This is your Lily saying so long to you. So long. So long. So long. So long. Have a happy, and so long. Till next week. Bye. So long. Bye. So long.

WEATHER ANNOUNCER And now, the weather.

SUSAN Well, as a matter of fact,
I got it on sale.

HAL If I had a place for it
everything would be fine.
Cake, Susan?

SUSAN (*to George*) Hal still
doesn't have a place.

GEORGE What kind of
place are you looking for?

HAL I'd like to find an
apartment with more than
one small room for under a
hundred dollars.

*Still without volume, an
advertisement for Miracle Headache
Pills: a woman is seen before and
after taking the pills.*

SUSAN Do you want to live in
the Village?

HAL Makes no difference.

GEORGE Don't live down there.

SUSAN Why not?

GEORGE It's too crowded.

SUSAN It's not so crowded, and
in the Village you can see a
lot of wonderful faces.

GEORGE Yes, well frankly I've
been working for a living for
twenty-one years and I resent
having to support a lot of
bums on relief.

SUSAN   That's not the Village.
That's the Bowery.

GEORGE   Let's not talk about it.

SUSAN   Why not?

GEORGE   I already told Hal that
people with differing points
of view shouldn't talk about
politics. And I shouldn't be
eating this cake either. (*snaps
volume on*)

*Lady Announcer begins to speak,
still without volume.*

LADY ANNOUNCER   And now
First Federal Savings and
Kennel-Heart Dog Food
present *Luncheon With
Carol,* a program especially
designed for the up-to-date
woman. Our topic for today:
I Quit. And here's Carol.

CAROL   Hello, ladies. This is
Carol. I have as my guest
today Mr. Ron Campbell,
just back from an eighteen-
month tour of duty in
Vietnam. Mr. Campbell was
a member of the famed
Green Berets. He is a holder
of the Bronze Star and the
South Vietnamese Order of
Merit; he has been nominated
for the U.S. Silver Star. A
few weeks ago he was offered
a field commission as captain.
But instead of accepting,
what did you do, Ron?

RON I quit.

CAROL That's right, you quit. Tell us why you quit, Ron, when you were obviously doing so well.

RON I didn't like being there.

CAROL You didn't?

RON No.

CAROL (*cheerfully*) I see.

RON We're committing mass murder.

CAROL (*interested*) Yes?

RON We're trying to take over a people that don't want to be taken over by anybody.

CAROL Now, Ron, American boys are out there dying so somebody must be doing something wrong somewhere.

RON Whoever in Hanoi or Peking or Washington is sending men out to be killed, *they're* doing something wrong.

CAROL (*interested in his opinion, tolerant*) I see.

RON You do? Well I was there for a year and a half and every day I saw things that would make you sick. Heads broken, babies smashed against walls—

CAROL (*deeply sympathetic*) I know.

RON You know?

CAROL War is horrible.

RON Listen—

CAROL Thank you, Ron. We've been talking this afternoon, ladies, with Ron Campbell, war hero.

RON Will you let me say something, please?

CAROL (*tolerating him, kindly*) And a fascinating talk it's been, Ron, but I'm afraid our time is up.

RON One—

CAROL (*with her special smile for the ladies*) Ladies, see you all tomorrow.

SUSAN (*dreamily*) I think I'm floating further and further left.

GEORGE You don't know a thing about it.

SUSAN I was listening to Norman Thomas last night—

LADY ANNOUNCER   This
program was brought to you
by First Federal Savings and
Kennel Heart Dog Food.
The opinions expressed on
this program are not
necessarily those of anyone
connected with it. A dog in
the home means a dog with
a heart.

GEORGE   I'm going to the men's
room.

LADY ANNOUNCER   Kennel-
Heart. Bow-wow. Wow.

SUSAN   Poor George.

HAL   You still haven't told me
about tonight.

*A very English man and a very
English woman appear in the
movie.*

SUSAN   Told you what about
tonight?

HE   Sarah.

SHE   Yes, Richard.

HAL   Are we going to the
movies or are we not going
to the movies?

HE   Our old apartment.

SUSAN   I don't know. I can't
make up my mind.

SHE   Yes, Richard. It's still
here.

HAL That's just fine.

HE It seems very small to me.

SHE It does to me, too.

SUSAN I want to work on my apartment.

HAL Okay.

HE Do you think we can live in it again?

SHE Not in the old way.

SUSAN I should really get it done.

HE In a better way.

HAL You're right.

SHE You've changed too, Richard, for the better.

HE So have you, darling, for the better.

SUSAN Suppose I let you know by the end of the afternoon?

SHE I've learned a lot.

HAL Suppose we forget I ever suggested it.

HE Maybe that's what war is for.

The people on television hum "White Cliffs of Dover" under the following.

SHE The brick wall in front of the window is gone.

HE We'll rebuild for the future.

SUSAN Oh, all right, I'll go. Happy?

HAL I'm so happy I could put a bullet through my brain.

SHE I hope there is never any more war. Ever, ever again.

HE Amen.

The people on television sing, meaningfully, the last line of "White Cliffs of Dover": "Tomorrow, just you wait and see."

SUSAN Sugar?

HAL You're like my grandmother.

First news announcer appears.

SUSAN How?

HAL She asked me if I took sugar every day we lived together. It was very comforting,

FIRST NEWS ANNOUNCER Baseball's Greg Pironelli, fifty-six, died today of a heart attack in St. Petersburg, Florida. He hit a total of four hundred and eighty home runs and had a lifetime batting average of three-forty-one.

HAL "Hal," she used to say to me, my grandmother, "you're going to be a big man."

100

HAL "Everybody's going to love you." She used to sing that song to me: "Poppa's gonna buy you a dog named Rover, and if that doggie doesn't bark, Poppa's gonna buy you a looking glass, and if that looking glass should break, you're still the sweetest little boy in town."

FIRST NEWS ANNOUNCER In 1963, the year he was elected to baseball's Hall of Fame in Cooperstown, New York, Pironelli suffered his first stroke. Pironelli owned a Florida-wide chain of laundries.

JOHNNY We're back.

SUSAN That's nice.

George enters and goes directly to telephone.

JOHNNY That's a very pretty dress you've got on, Luci.

LUCI Why, thank you, Johnny.

GEORGE Hello, dear? I've gotten out of the midnight-to-three shift.

JOHNNY Nice having you with us, Luci.

LUCI Nice being here, Johnny.

GEORGE Isn't that wonderful news?

JOHNNY Do you miss your father, Luci ? Now you're living in Austin?

LUCI   Oh sure. I miss him.
Now I'm livin' in Austin.

GEORGE   My stomach is killing
me.

JOHNNY   Does your father ever
ask your advice about
important matters, Luci?

George is finding a pencil.

LUCI   Well, Johnny, one day I
told him good and proper
what I thought of all those
nervous Nellies interferin'
with my daddy's war.

JOHNNY   And what did he say?

LUCI   He laughed.

GEORGE   (*writing*)   Cauliflower.

JOHNNY   I guess he must worry
a lot about the war.

GEORGE   Mayonnaise.

LUCI   Oh, he worries.

GEORGE   Large soap-cream.
Why large? No, I don't care.
I was just wondering.

LUCI   One night he said to me,
"Luci, darlin', your daddy
may go down in history
as the man who started
World War Three."

GEORGE   Toothpaste.

JOHNNY   What did you say to
him, Luci?

LUCI "Daddy," I said, "let us
pray. Right here on the floor
of the Oval Room."

JOHNNY What did you pray
for, Luci?

GEORGE Listen, honey, I love
you. You know that, don't
you?

LUCI Johnny, we prayed for
our boys to stay safe in the
war, for my daddy to receive
divine guidance, we prayed
for total victory and for just
about everything.

GEORGE No, I have not been
drinking and it's rotten of you
to ask.

JOHNNY It's nice talkin' to
you, Luci.

GEORGE Okay, okay, I'm sorry.

LUCI It's nice talkin' to you
too, Johnny.

GEORGE (*hanging up*) Good-bye.

JOHNNY We'll be back.

SUSAN Have a little coffee,
George.

GEORGE No, thanks.

HAL Oh, come on, George,
have a little coffee.

GEORGE A sip.

SUSAN Sugar or saccharine?

GEORGE Sugar.

SUSAN George.

GEORGE Don't take care of me.
I said sugar.

SUSAN Whatever you want,
George.

*An Evangelist appears with his
choir, which is singing "Onward
Christian Soldiers."*

EVANGELIST If we could look
through the ceiling of this
wonderful new air-
conditioned stadium we
could see the stars. Nonethe-
less I have heard them
in faraway countries, I have
heard them criticize,
criticize us and the
leaders we know and love.

SUSAN George, what are
you eating now?

GEORGE Chicken sandwich.

SUSAN Give me a bite.

*Hal plays with his penknife. Susan
eats another piece of cake. George
eats his chicken sandwich.*

EVANGELIST Why? Well I will
tell you why. They criticize
us because we are rich, as if
money itself were an evil.
Money, the Bible says, is the
root of evil, not evil itself. I
have seen a roomful of men
and women, powerful
Hollywood celebrities at four

George starts to cough.

SUSAN   What's the matter, George?

George motions her away and continues to cough.

HAL (*turning volume off*)   Spit it out, George.

SUSAN   Hal, leave him alone.

HAL   George, spit it out.
(*He thumps George on the back.*)

SUSAN   Hal! George, is it epilepsy?

HAL   It's something in his throat.

SUSAN   Try to tell us what it is, George.

HAL and **GEORGE** (*together*)
Chicken!

HAL   He has a chicken bone stuck in his throat.

SUSAN   Oh my God. Well give him some water.

o'clock A.M. in the morning, listening to me with tears streaming down their faces crying out to me that they had lost touch with God.

EVANGELIST   "In God We Trust" is on our coins, ladies and gentlemen—

The Evangelist's choir sings "Onward Christian Soldiers."

George's choking is getting worse.

HAL Water will wash right by it.
Let me look. (*He holds
George's head and looks into his
mouth.*) Don't move, George.
I want to take a look (*looks in
George's mouth*). There it is.

SUSAN (*also looking*) Ugh, it's
stuck in his throat. I'll get
some water.

*Hal and Susan let go of George,
who falls to the floor.*

HAL Not water.

SUSAN Why not?

HAL Because water will wash
right past the thing. It needs
something to push it out.

SUSAN Like what?

HAL Like bread.

SUSAN Bread? Bread will get
stuck on the bone and he'll
choke.

HAL You're wrong.

SUSAN I'm right.

HAL Bread will push it right
down.

SUSAN Water will do that.

HAL You're wrong.

SUSAN It's you that's wrong and won't admit it.

HAL I'm going to give him some bread.

SUSAN I won't allow it.

HAL *You* won't allow it?

SUSAN It'll kill him.

HAL He's choking right now and I'm going to give him some of this bread.

SUSAN Give him water.

HAL I said bread.

SUSAN *(starting to walk past Hal)* And I said water.

HAL *(grabbing her arm)* Bread.

SUSAN Water. Ow, you're hurting me.

George is having a very bad time. Hal and Susan turn to look at him, speaking softly.

SUSAN Let's call the operator.

HAL It would take too long.

SUSAN And he wouldn't like anyone to see him.

HAL Why not?

SUSAN I don't know.

At this point George finally coughs the thing up. His cough subsides into an animal pant.

SUSAN (*going to him, patting him*)
  Poor George.

HAL   It's over.

SUSAN   No thanks to you.

HAL   Nor you.

SUSAN (*putting George's head on her breast*)   He might have choked. Poor George.

GEORGE (*pushing her away*)   Fuck!

George lurches against the console on his way to the bathroom, accidentally turning up the volume.

EVANGELIST'S CHOIR (*still singing "Onward Christian Soldiers"*)   With the cross of Jesus—

Hal changes channels from the Evangelist's meeting to "My Favorite Teenager."

SUSAN (*sitting in her chair*)   Poor George.

MOTHER   Why aren't you going?

DAUGHTER (*sitting in George's chair at the control console*)

Because I told Harold Sternpepper he could take me.

MOTHER Yes, and—

DAUGHTER Well, Harold Sternpepper is a creep. Everybody knows that.

The remaining people on television make the sound of canned laughter.

HAL (*sitting in his chair*) What movie are we going to?

MOTHER So, why—

DAUGHTER Oh, because I was mad at Gail.

Canned laughter.

SUSAN I don't know.

MOTHER What about Johnny Beaumont?

HAL What about George?

SUSAN What about him?

DAUGHTER What about him?

HAL Well, I guess it's none of my business.

MOTHER Well, I guess it's none of my business.

GEORGE (*returning*) What's the matter?

FATHER What's the matter?

SUSAN Nothing.

DAUGHTER Nothing.

GEORGE Going somewhere?

FATHER Why aren't you dressed for the prom?

DAUGHTER I'm not going to the prom.

SUSAN We're going to the movies.

FATHER Why not? Why isn't she going, Grace?

MOTHER Don't ask me. I just live here.

Hal and Susan and George are slowing down because they are mesmerized by "My Favorite Teenager."

Canned laughter.

GEORGE What movie are you going to?

FATHER Why doesn't anybody tell me anything around here?

Canned laughter.

DAUGHTER (*getting up from George's chair*) Oh, why don't you two leave me alone. I'm not going because nobody's taking me.

GEORGE Mind if I come along?

FATHER (*sitting in George's chair*) Nobody's taking my little girl to the junior prom? I'll take her myself.

SUSAN Oh, George, you don't really want to.

DAUGHTER (*stifling a yelp of horror*) Oh no, Daddy, don't bother. I mean how would it look, I mean—

GEORGE I'd be pleased as punch.

FATHER I'd be pleased as punch.

DAUGHTER (*aside to Mother*) Help.

Canned laughter.

SUSAN   Hal, say something.

MOTHER *(to Father)*   Now,
   dear, don't you think
   for your age—

Canned laughter.

HAL *(to George)*   You look
   bushed to me, George.

GEORGE   Who's bushed?

FATHER   My age?

Canned laughter.

FATHER *(standing and doing a two-
   step)*   I'd like to see anybody
   laugh at my two-step.

George sits in his chair.

Canned laughter.

DAUGHTER *(in despair)*   Oh,
   Daddy. Mother, *do*
   something.

*Hal, Susan and
George are completely
mesmerized by the
television show.*

Canned laughter.

MOTHER *(putting her arm around
   George's shoulder)*   I think it's
   a very nice idea. And maybe
   I'll go with Harold
   Sternpepper.

Canned laughter.

DAUGHTER *(loudly, sitting on
   Hal's knee)*   Oh, Mother,
   oh, Daddy, oh no!

The canned laughter mounts and
the "My Favorite Teenager"
music comes on.

Now they all speak like situation-comedy characters.

HAL   What movie shall we go to?

GEORGE   Let's talk about it over
dinner.

HAL.   Who said anything about
dinner?

All of the people on television do
canned laughter now. They are
crowded around the control console.

SUSAN   Isn't anybody going to
ask me what I want to do?

Canned laughter.

GEORGE   Sure, what do you
want, Susan?

HAL   It's up to you.

SUSAN   Well, have I got a
surprise for you two. *I'm*
going home to fix up my
apartment and you two can
have dinner to-*gether.*

Hal, Susan and George join in the canned laughter. Then, lights off.
Curtain call: all are in the same position, silent, their faces frozen into
laughing masks.

CURTAIN

MOTEL
A MASQUE FOR THREE DOLLS

photo by Phill Niblock

In the 1964–65 season *Motel* as a single play (which was originally called *The Savage God* and then *America Hurrah*) premiered at LaMama ETC, in New York City, directed by Michael Kahn and with doll heads by Robert Wilson, and toured in Europe.

The actors in the dolls in the 1966 Pocket Theatre production were as follows:

MOTEL-KEEPER: Brenda Smiley

MAN: Conard Fowkes

WOMAN: James Barbosa

MOTEL-KEEPER'S VOICE: Ruth White

MUSIC: Marianne de Pury

. . . after all our subtle colour and nervous rhythm, after the faint mixed tints of Conder, what more is possible? After us the Savage God.

YEATS

Lights come up on the motel-keeper doll. The intensity of the light will increase as the play continues.

The motel-keeper doll is large, much larger than human size, but the impression of hugeness can come mainly from the fact that her head is at least three times larger than would be normal in proportion to her body. She is all gray. She has a large full skirt which reaches to the floor. She has squarish breasts. The hair curlers on her head suggest electronic receivers.

The motel-keeper doll has eyeglasses which are mirrors. It doesn't matter what these mirrors reflect at any given moment. The audience may occasionally catch a glimpse of itself, or be bothered by reflections of light in the mirrors. It doesn't matter; the sensory nerves of the audience are not to be spared.

The motel room in which the motel-keeper doll stands is anonymously modern, except for certain "homey" touches. A neon light blinks outside the window. The colors in the room, like the colors in the clothes on the man and woman dolls, are violent combinations of oranges, pinks and reds against a reflective plastic background.

The motel-keeper's voice, which never stops, comes from a loudspeaker, or from several loudspeakers in the theater. The voice will be, at first, mellow and husky, and then, as the light grows harsher and brighter, the voice will grow harsher too, more set in its pattern, hard finally, and patronizing and petty.

An actor on platform shoes works the motel-keeper doll from inside it. The actor can move the doll's arms only or its entire body. As the voice begins, the arms move, and then the motel-keeper doll fusses about the room in little circles.

MOTEL-KEEPER'S VOICE   I am old. I am an old idea: the walls; that from which it springs forth. I enclose the nothing, making then a place in which it happens. I am the room: a Roman theater where cheers break loose the lion; a railroad carriage in the forest

115

at Compiègne, in 1918, and in 1941. I have been rooms of marble and rooms of cork, all letting forth an avalanche. Rooms of mud and rooms of silk. This room will be slashed too, as if by a scimitar, its contents spewed and yawned out. That is what happens. It is almost happening, in fact. I am this room.

The doors at the back of the room open and headlights shine into the eyes of the audience; passing in front of the headlights, in silhouette, we see two more huge dolls, the man and the woman. The motel-keeper's voice continues.

MOTEL-KEEPER'S VOICE   It's nice; not so fancy as some, but with all the conveniences. And a touch of home. The antimacassar comes from my mother's house in Boise. Boise, Idaho. Sits kind of nice, I think, on the Swedish swing. That's my own idea, you know. All modern, up-to-date, that's it—no motel on this route is more up-to-date. Or cleaner. Go look, then talk me a thing or two.

The woman doll enters. Her shoulders are thrown way back, like a girl posing for a calendar. Her breasts are particularly large and perfect, wiggleable if possible. She has a cherry-lipstick smile, blonde hair and a garish patterned dress. Both the man and the woman dolls are the same size as the motel-keeper doll, with heads at least three times larger than would be normal proportionately. The man and the woman dolls, however, are flesh-colored and have more mobility. The actors inside these dolls are also on platform shoes. There is absolutely no rapport between the motel-keeper and the man and woman. All of the motel-keeper's remarks are addressed generally. She is never directly motivated by the actions of the man and woman dolls.

As the woman doll enters, she puts down her purse and inspects the room. Then she takes off her dress, revealing lace panties and a bra.

MOTEL-KEEPER'S VOICE   All modern here but, as I say, with the tang of home. Do you understand? When folks are fatigued, in a strange place? Not that it's old-fashioned. No. Not in the wrong way. There's a button-push here for TV. The toilet flushes of its own accord. All you've got to do is get off. Pardon my mentioning it, but you'll have to go far before you see a thing like that on this route. Oh, it's quite a room. Yes. And reasonable. Sign here. Pardon the pen leak. I can see you're fatigued.

The woman doll goes into the bathroom.

MOTEL-KEEPER'S VOICE   Any children? Well, that's nice. Children
don't appreciate travel. And rooms don't appreciate children. As
it happens it's the last one I've got left. I'll just flip my vacancy
switch. Twelve dollars, please. In advance that'll be. That way
you can go any time you want to go, you know, get an early
start. On a trip to see sights, are you? That's nice. You just get
your luggage while I unlock the room. You can see the light.

*The man doll enters carrying a suitcase. He has a cigar and a loud Florida
shirt. He closes the door, inspects the room and takes off his clothes, except
for his loudly patterned shorts.*

MOTEL-KEEPER'S VOICE   There now. What I say doesn't matter.
You can see. It speaks for itself. The room speaks for itself. You
can see it's a perfectly modern room. But a taste of home. I've
seen to that. A taste of home. Comfy, cozy, nice, but a taste of
newness. That's what. You can see it.
     The best stop on Route Six Sixty-six. Well, there might be
others like it, but this is the best stop. You've arrived at the right
place. This place. And a hooked rug. I don't care what, but I've
said no room *is* without a hooked rug.

Sound of the toilet flushing.

MOTEL-KEEPER'S VOICE   No complaints yet. Never. Modern
people like modern places. Oh yes. I can tell. They tell me. And
reasonable. Very very reasonable rates. No cheaper rates on the
route, not for this. You receive what you pay for.

Sound of the toilet flushing again.

MOTEL-KEEPER'S VOICE   All that driving and driving and driving.
Fatigued. You must be. I would be. Miles and miles and miles.

*The man doll begins an inspection of the bed. He pulls at the bedspread,
testing its strength.*

MOTEL-KEEPER'S VOICE Fancy. Fancy your ending up right here. You didn't know and I didn't know. But you did. End up right here. Respectable and decent and homelike. Right here.

The woman doll comes back from the bathroom to get her negligee from her purse. She returns to the bathroom.

MOTEL-KEEPER'S VOICE All folks everywhere sitting in the very palm of God. Waiting, whither, whence.

The man doll pulls the bedspread, blankets and sheets off the bed, tearing them apart. He jumps hard on the bed.

MOTEL-KEEPER'S VOICE Any motel you might have come to on Six Sixty-six. Any motel. On that vast network of roads. Whizzing by, whizzing by. Trucks too. And cars from everywhere. Full up with folks, all sitting in the very palm of God. I can tell proper folks when I get a look at them. All folks.

The man doll rummages through the suitcase, throwing clothes about the room.

MOTEL-KEEPER'S VOICE Country roads, state roads, United States roads. It's a big world and here you are. I noticed you got a license plate. I've not been to there myself. I've not been to anywhere myself, excepting town for supplies, and Boise. Boise, Idaho.

Toilet articles and bathroom fixtures, including toilet paper and the toilet seat, are thrown out of the bathroom. The man doll casually tears pages out of the bible.

MOTEL-KEEPER'S VOICE The world arrives to me, you'd say. It's a small world. These plastic flowers here: "Made in Japan," on the label. You noticed? Got them from the catalogue. Cat-a-logue. Every product in this room is ordered.

The man doll pulls down some of the curtains. Objects continue to be thrown from the bathroom.

MOTEL-KEEPER'S VOICE Ordered from the catalogue. Excepting the antimacassar and the hooked rug. Made the hooked rug myself. Tang of home. No room is a room without. 'Course the bedspread, hand-hooked, hooked near here at town. Mrs. Harritt. Betsy Harritt gets materials through another catalogue. Cat-a-logue.

The woman doll comes out of the bathroom wearing her negligee over her panties and bra. When the man doll notices her, he stops his other activities and goes to her.

MOTEL-KEEPER'S VOICE Myself, I know it from the catalogue: bottles, bras, breakfasts, refrigerators, cast-iron gates, plastic posies,

The woman doll opens her negligee and the man doll pulls off her bra. The man and woman dolls embrace. The woman doll puts lipstick on her nipples.

MOTEL-KEEPER'S VOICE paper subscriptions, Buick trucks, blankets, forks, clitter-clack darning hooks, transistors and antimacassars, vinyl plastics,

The man doll turns on the TV. It glares viciously and plays loud rock-and-roll music.

MOTEL-KEEPER'S VOICE crazy quilts, paper hairpins, cats, catnip, club feet, canisters, banisters, holy books, tattooed toilet articles, tables, tea-cozies,

The man doll writes simple obscene words on the wall. The woman doll does the same with her lipstick.

MOTEL-KEEPER'S VOICE pickles, bayberry candles, South Dakotan Kewpie dolls, fiberglass hair, polished milk, amiable grandpappies, colts, Galsworthy books, cribs, cabinets, teeter-totters,

The woman doll has turned to picture-making. She draws a crude cock and coyly adds pubic hair and drops of come.

MOTEL-KEEPER'S VOICE   and television sets.
Oh I tell you it, I do. It's a wonder. Full with things, the world, full up. Shall I tell you my thought? Next year there's a shelter to be built by me, yes. Shelter motel. Everything to be placed under the ground. Signs up in every direction up and down Six Sixty-six.

The man and woman dolls dance.

MOTEL-KEEPER'S VOICE   Complete security, security while you sleep tight, bury your troubles at this motel, homelike, very comfy, and encased in lead, every room its own set, fourteen-day emergency supplies $5.00 extra,

The rock-and-roll music gets louder and louder. A civil-defense siren, one long wail, begins to build. The man and woman dolls proceed methodically to greater and greater violence. They smash the TV screen and picture frames. They pull down the remaining curtains, smash the window, throw bits of clothing and bedding around, and finally tear off the arms of the Motel-keeper doll.

MOTEL-KEEPER'S VOICE   Self-contained latrine waters, filters, counters, periscopes and mechanical doves, hooked rugs, dearest little picture frames for loved ones—made in Japan—through the catalogue. Cat-a-logue. You can pick items and products: cablecackles—so nice—cuticles, twice-twisted combs with corrugated calisthenics, meat-beaters, fish-tackles, bug bombs, toasted terra-cottad Tanganyikan switchblades, ochre closets, ping-pong balls, didies, Capricorn and Cancer prognostics, crackers, total uppers, stickpins, basting tacks . . .

The motel-keeper's voice is drowned out by the other sounds—siren and music—which have built to a deafening pitch and come from all parts of the theater. The door opens again and headlights shine into the eyes of the audience.
The actor inside the motel-keeper doll has slipped out of it.
The man and woman dolls tear off the head of the motel-keeper doll, then throw her body aside.

Then, one by one, the man and woman dolls leave the motel room and walk down the aisle. Fans blow air through the debacle on stage onto the audience.

After an instant more of excruciatingly loud noise: blackout and silence.

It is suggested that the actors do not take a bow after this play.

CURTAIN

THE SERPENT
A CEREMONY

photo by Bergh and Tornberg

The Serpent, created with the Open Theater ensemble, directed by Joseph Chaikin, premiered May 2, 1968, at the Teatro Degli Arte in Rome. It toured Europe before opening in New York City. The actors: Joyce Aaron, James Barbosa, Raymond Barry, Jenn Ben-Yakov, Shami Chaikin, Brenda Dixon, Ron Faber, Cynthia Harris, Philip Harris, Jayne Haynes, Ralph Lee, Dorothy Lyman, Peter Maloney, Ellen Schindler, Tina Shepard, Barbara Vann, Lee Worley and Paul Zimet. Costumes by Gwen Rabericant.

The Serpent is dedicated to the memory of Roger H. Klein.

WARM-UP AND PROCESSION

In all parts of the theater, including the aisle, the actors warm up. Each does what physical exercises best prepare him or her for playing. The lights dim slowly and not completely. Each actor wears a costume that seems natural on her or him particularly, of colorful and easily falling materials that flatter the movement of his body. The total effect, when the company moves together, is kaleidoscopic. The actress who will play Eve wears a simply cut short white dress. Adam wears old khaki pants and a shirt with no collar. None of the others is costumed for a particular role.

After a few minutes the actors begin to move around the theater in a procession led by an actor who taps out a simple marching rhythm on a bongo drum. The players don't use their voices, but they explore every other sound that can be made by the human body—slapping oneself, pounding one's chest, etc. The actors also use simple and primitive musical instruments during the procession. During some later scenes an actor may accompany the stage action with the repeated sound of a single note on one of these instruments. The procession appears to be one of medieval mummers. All at once all stop in a freeze. This happens three times during the procession. During a freeze each actor portrays one of various possible motifs from the play, such as: the sheep, the serpent, the President's wife's reaching gesture, Adam's movement, Cain's waiting movement, Eve's movement, the heron and the old people. In countries outside the United States where it is thought that not everyone will immediately recognize all events in the piece, at these motif moments actors shout out the names King and Kennedy.

Transitions from one scene to the next will be done rhythmically, in the character of either of the two scenes, as a slow transformation or "dissolve," or completely out of character, with the audience merely watching the actor go to his next place. Each transition is slightly different, but predetermined.

THE DOCTOR

*When the procession is nearly over, the doctor detaches himself from it.
From among the actors, a female victim is carried over by two actors and
placed on a table formed by three other actors. The doctor stands behind the
table. He speaks in a kind of chant. His movements are slow and ritualistic.
The rest of the actors, watching, will provide stylized sounds for the
operation. A gunshot will be heard once in a while. We will have already
heard the gunshot a couple of times during the end of the procession.*

DOCTOR   Autopsy.
   With a single stroke of the cleaver,
   The corpse is split open.

Actors make cutting sound from the backs of their throats.

   The fatty tissues
   Fall away
   In two yellow folds.

DOCTOR   In a corpse
   The blood is black
   And does not flow.
   In a living person
   The blood is black
   And flows
   From the liver
   To the spine, and from
   There to the heart
   And the brain.
   To penetrate the skull
   We shave the head,
   And cut out a disk of flesh
   The shape of a half moon.

Actors make the sound of the saw.

   We inject the exposed bone
   With a steel needle,

126

And push air into the skull
To look into the brain.
Then, with a diamond drill,
We enter the bone.

Actors make the sound of teeth nibbling.

And nibble at the opening
With a hammer, chisel and knife.
The brain is cream-colored.
It is a balance of chemicals.
Thought is effected
By traveling electrons.

Gunshot

During a brain operation,
Pressing at this point
With a knife
Causes live patients
To exclaim at sudden memories.
If we press here,
We get fear.

Gunshot

*The patient, who so far has been lying fairly still, climbs off the table
and comes slowly toward the audience in a state of extreme bodily tension,
making a soundless appeal.*

In gunshot wounds
Infection ensues
Unless an operation
Is undertaken immediately.
We excise the wound,
And suck out bits of bone
And diffluent brain matter.
If the patient survives,
He may live for weeks
Or months
Or years.

The four women of the chorus make the same small long scream at the backs of their throats that they will make when we later see Abel's ghost.

He functions barely.
He is unconscious.
Or semiconscious.
We don't know.
We clean him,
And feed him.
But there is no measure
To what degree
The mind imagines, receives or dreams.

KENNEDY-KING ASSASSINATION

A cheering crowd forms in a semicircle at the back of the stage. Using four chairs, or sitting on the floor if the stage is raked enough, four actors, two men and two women, sit in the car as the central characters in the assassination of President John F. Kennedy. The governor and his wife are in front. The President and his wife are in the backseat exactly as in all the newspaper pictures. They are waving. The crowd, moving from one side of the stage to the other behind them, gives the same impression of movement as in a film when the scenery is moved behind what is supposed to be a "moving" car. When the crowd moves the first time, one figure is left to the side: the assassin. Another figure stands behind the crowd, and does not move with it. Again, everyone but the people in the car is facing the audience. The people in the car look at the audience, smile at them as if they were the crowd. The events which are the actual assassination are broken down into a count of twelve, as if seen on a slowed-down silent film. Within this count all the things which we are told factually happened, happen:

   1: *All four wave.*
   2: *President is shot in the neck.*

3: *Governor is shot in the shoulder.*

4: *President is shot in the head. Governor's wife pulls her husband down and covers him with her body.*

5: *President falls against his wife.*

6: *President's wife begins to register that something is wrong. She looks at her husband.*

7: *She puts her hands on his head.*

8: *She lifts her knee to put his head on it.*

9: *She looks into the front seat.*

10: *She begins to realize horror.*

11: *She starts to get up.*

12: *She begins to crawl out the back of the open car, and to reach out her hand.*

Immediately after that, the numbers are started again. The numbers have been shouted aloud by guards who come down toward the front of the stage and kneel, their backs to the audience. Then the count is made a third time, backward this time. The crowd reactions are also backward, as if a film of these events were being run backward. Then the guards call out numbers from one to twelve at random, and the people in the crowd, as well as the characters in the car, assume the positions they had at the time of the number being called. The blank-faced assassin has simply mimed shooting a rifle at the count of two. He faces the audience too. The action in the car continues, as if the count from one to twelve were going on perpetually, but we no longer hear the guards shouting. The crowd, aside from the assassin, forms a tight group at the rear of the right side of the stage. They face the audience. The four women of the chorus are in the front. The crowd shouts and marches very slowly toward the front.

At first we do not understand what they are shouting. The shout is broken down into first vowels, second vowels, center consonants and end consonants. Each of four sections of the crowd shows one part. The shout is repeated four times, each time adding one of the four parts.

CROWD SHOUT   I was not involved.

I am a small person.

I hold no opinions.
I stay alive.

Everyone on stage freezes, and the figure at the back quietly speaks words of Dr. Martin Luther King:

KING   Though we stand in life at midnight,
I have a dream.
He's allowed me
To go to the mountaintop,
And I've looked over.
I've seen the promised land.
I have a dream
That we are, as always,
On the threshold of a new dawn,
And that we shall all see it together.

The crowd continues its shout, building up these stanzas as it did the previous ones, but the words are still not completely clear. The characters in the car continue their slow-motion actions.

CROWD SHOUT   I mind my own affairs.
I am a little man.
I lead a private life.
I stay alive.

I'm no assassin.
I'm no president.
I don't know who did the killing.
I stay alive.

I keep out of big affairs.
I am not a violent man.
I am very sorry, still
I stay alive.

At times we have been able to make out the words of the President's wife which she has been speaking on count twelve as she reaches out.

PRESIDENT'S WIFE   I've got his brains in my—

The last time through the whole shout, we hear each section of the crowd emphasizing its own part, while the assassin, who has been standing on one side, facing the audience and going through, silently, the agonies of having been himself shot, speaks the words with the others, clearly.

CROWD AND ASSASSIN   I was not involved.
  I am a small person.
  I hold no opinions.
  I stay alive.

  I mind my own affairs.
  I am a little man.
  I lead a private life.
  I stay alive.

  I'm no assassin.
  I'm no president.
  I don't know who did the killing.
  I stay alive.

  I keep out of big affairs.
  I am not a violent man.
  I am very sorry, still
  I stay alive.

THE GARDEN

Everyone's breath comes short and heavy and rhythmically, as if in surprise. The four chorus women dressed in black detach themselves from the rest of the group and in short spurts of movement and speech go to the downstage right area, facing the audience.

FIRST WOMAN OF THE CHORUS   I no longer live in the beginning.

SECOND WOMAN OF THE CHORUS   I've lost the beginning.

THIRD WOMAN OF THE CHORUS   I'm in the middle,
  Knowing.

THIRD AND FOURTH WOMEN OF THE CHORUS Neither the end
  Nor the beginning.

FIRST WOMAN I'm in the middle.

SECOND WOMAN Coming from the beginning.

THIRD AND FOURTH WOMEN And going toward the end.

*In the meantime, others are forming the creatures in the Garden of Eden.
Many of the creatures are personal, previously selected by each actor as
expressing an otherwise inexpressible part of himself or herself. For the
audience, perhaps the heron has the most identifiable reality. He moves
about gently, tall, proud, in slow spurts; he stands on one foot, moves his
wings slightly, occasionally, and makes a soft "brrring" noise. Other
creatures become distinguishable. The serpent is formed by five (male) actors
all writhing together in a group, their arms, legs, hands, tongues all
moving.*

  *The chorus women repeat their "in the beginning" lines. They speak
these thoughts as a secret to the audience.*

  *There is a sense of awe about the whole creation of the garden. The two
human creatures also become discernible. As Eve sits up and sees the world,
she screams in amazement. The sound of her scream is actually made by
one of the four chorus women. They are also Eve. They think of themselves
as one person, and any one of them at this moment might reflect Eve.*

  *Adam falls asleep. The heron and the serpent are now more clearly
discernible from the other creatures. The creatures play quietly, in awe. The
serpent is feeling out the environment with hands and mouths and fingers.
There is nothing orgiastic about the garden—on the contrary, there is the
restraint of curious animals in a strange environment.*

SERPENT 1 Is it true?

SERPENT 2 Is it true?

SERPENT 3 That you and he,

SERPENT 4 You and he

SERPENT 4 and 5 May do anything?

SERPENT 2   Anything in the garden you want to do?

SERPENT 1   Is that true?

EVE   We may do anything
Except one thing.

FIRST WOMAN OF THE CHORUS   We may do anything
Except one thing.

In the dialogue between Eve and the serpent, the first of the chorus women echoes Eve's lines, but with the emphasis placed on different words. The four chorus women look at the audience as if it were the serpent in front of them. The serpent speaks and hisses to Eve with all his five mouths. Care must be taken by the actors playing the serpent that all the words are heard distinctly, despite overlap in speaking. Eve is in a state of tremor at being alive. The serpent is seducing her with his even greater aliveness, as well as with the intellectual argument. As Eve comes closer to being in the state the serpent is in, her movements begin to imitate the serpent's, and she, finally, is seducing him, too. Some of the other actors are now seated on a bench facing the audience at the back of the stage, where they rest and pay attention to the action. This bench is where those who are not playing a particular scene will always go—none of the actors will ever actually leave the stage. During Eve's dialogue with the serpent, only the heron and one or two other animals in the garden are upright, but they do not distract us. The serpent is not only the serpent, he is also the tree, and he holds apples.

SERPENT 2   What one thing?

EVE   We are not allowed to eat from the tree.

FIRST WOMAN   We are not allowed
To eat from the tree.

SERPENT 3   Not allowed to eat?

EVE   We may not even touch it.

WOMAN   We may not even touch it.

SERPENT 1   Not even touch?

SERPENT 4 and 5   Not touch?

SERPENT 5   Why not even touch?

EVE   Adam said I would die.

WOMAN   Adam said I would die.

The serpent is gently surrounding Eve until she has touched him without realizing it.

SERPENT 3   If you—

SERPENT 4   If you touch—

SERPENT 4 and 5   If you touch the tree—

SERPENT 1   Adam said

SERPENT 2   If you touch the tree—

SERPENT 4 and 5   If you even touch the tree
   You will die—

SERPENT 1   But—

SERPENT 2   But—

SERPENT 3   But—

Eve realizes her back is against the tree.

SERPENT 5   Have you died?

SERPENT 4 (*whispering*)   Have you died?

EVE   I don't know.

WOMAN   I don't know.

SERPENT 2   You touched the tree.

SERPENT 2 and 3   And you haven't died.

SERPENT 4   You haven't died.

EVE   But Adam said—

WOMAN   But Adam said—

SERPENT 1   Oh, Adam said,

SERPENT 2   Adam said, Adam said . . .

SERPENT 1 and 2   Listen.

SERPENT 2 and 3   Answer me this.

SERPENT 5 (*overlapping the others*)   This.

SERPENT 4   Could it?

SERPENT 3   Could it hurt more
To eat than to touch?

SERPENT 5   To eat than to touch?

SERPENT 1   Could it?

EVE   It is forbidden.

WOMAN   It is forbidden.

SERPENT 2   Who has forbidden it?

SERPENT 1   Who?

EVE   God.

WOMAN   God.

SERPENT 4   And why?

SERPENT 5   Why has he forbidden it?

SERPENT 4   Why?

SERPENT 3   Why does he set limits

SERPENT 2 and 3   Against you and Adam?

SERPENT 1   Think.

SERPENT 2   Is the fruit God's property?

SERPENT 3   Is it?

SERPENT 1   He says Adam and Eve may not eat.
But are Adam and Eve
Guests in this garden?

SERPENT 2   Are they guests?

SERPENT 1   Don't they live here?

SERPENT 3   May they not eat where they want?

EVE (*turning away*)   I don't know.

WOMAN   I don't know.

SERPENT 5   Also, also haven't you

SERPENT 4 and 5   Haven't you noticed

SERPENT 4   That the younger always have rule
Over the elder creation?

SERPENT 2   Haven't you noticed,
and aren't you afraid?

SERPENT 1   Aren't you afraid
And hadn't you better hurry

SERPENT 1 and 2   And eat the fruit now
Before the next comes to rule
Over you?

EVE   I'm not afraid.

WOMAN   I'm not afraid.

SERPENT (*to itselves*) 1   She's not afraid.

SERPENT 2   Why should she be?

SERPENT 3   How could she be?

SERPENT 4 How?

SERPENT 5 She couldn't be,
She doesn't know.

SERPENT 4 Doesn't know what?

SERPENT 3 Doesn't know she exists.

SERPENT 4 Why doesn't she know it?

SERPENT 3 Because she hasn't eaten.

SERPENT 2 If she'd eaten, she'd know.

SERPENT 1 Know what?

SERPENT 4 What worlds she would know
If she ate.

SERPENT 5 What worlds?

SERPENT 1 If she ate she would know

SERPENT 1 and 2 And if she knew

SERPENT 1 and 2 and 3 She could—

EVE What?

WOMAN What?

SERPENT 4 You don't know

SERPENT 5 Because you haven't eaten.

EVE Do you know?

WOMAN Do you know?

SERPENT 2 I don't know.

SERPENT 1 I don't.

SERPENT 3 But I can imagine.

SERPENT 4   Imagine.

SERPENT 5   Imagine.

EVE   But, is what you can imagine
What will be?

WOMAN   But, is what you can imagine
What will be?

SERPENT 1 and 2   How can you know
Until you eat?

SERPENT 5   How can I know?

SERPENT 4   How can I know until you eat?

SERPENT 1   This garden,

SERPENT 2   All these animals and these plants—

SERPENT 2 and 3   Were once only imagined.

EVE   Shall I risk losing all these?

WOMAN   Shall I risk losing all these?

SERPENT 1   It may be.

SERPENT 2   It may be that no garden

SERPENT 4   Is better than this one.

SERPENT 5   This garden.

SERPENT 4   It may be.

SERPENT 2   But you won't know,

SERPENT 1   You can't know
Until you eat.

SERPENT 2   How could you know?

EVE   If I eat
   And if I die
   Will you die too?

WOMAN   If I eat
   And if I die
   Will you die too?

SERPENT 1   If you die,
   I will die too.

EVE   Why do you want me to eat?

WOMAN   Why do you want me to eat?

SERPENT 5   Because I want—

SERPENT 4   I want to—

SERPENT 3   I want to know.

EVE   Know what?

WOMAN   Know what?

SERPENT 2   Know what you will know.

SERPENT 1   Know what will happen.

EVE   I might.
   I might do it.
   I might do it if God didn't know.

WOMAN   I might.
   I might do it.
   I might do it if God didn't know.

SERPENT 3   You might—

SERPENT 4   Might do it if God didn't know?

SERPENT 2   But you want to.

SERPENT 1   And he knows you want to.

SERPENT 5   Is a crime

SERPENT 4   Only a crime

SERPENT 5   When you're caught?

EVE   Shall I do what I want to then?

WOMAN   Shall I do what I want to then?

SERPENT 1 and 2 and 3 and 4 and 5   Yes!

EVE   Even if what I want is to listen
   To God and not to you?

WOMAN   Even if what I want is to listen
   To God and not to you?

SERPENT 1   Yes.

SERPENT 2   If you want.

SERPENT 3 and 4   If you want.

SERPENT 5   Yes.

EVE   Then I will eat.

WOMAN   Then I will eat.

She bites into one of the apples held by the many hands of the serpent.

EVE   Because I want to.

WOMAN   Because I want to.

EATING THE APPLE

When Eve finally eats she is seated in the middle of the serpent. After a couple of frantic bites, there is a pause as Eve begins to savor the experience. The first woman of the chorus, who echoed Eve's words to the serpent, now describes Eve's experience.

FIRST WOMAN OF THE CHORUS And Eve looked
At the creatures in the garden,
And at the ground
And at the wind and the water,
And she said: I am not the same as these.
And she began to examine
Her skin and her eyes
And her ears and her nose and her mouth.
And she began to examine her own mind.
And Eve went to Adam
To persuade him to eat.
But Adam said:
"You have eaten of that which was forbidden, and you shall die.
Do you want me to eat and die too?"

Eve in a kind of frenzy has gone over to Adam, woken him up, and is trying to have him eat. He, at first, refuses but then is caught up in her frenzy and he eats too. After his first bite nothing seems to happen. The serpent freezes during Adam and Eve's argument but he has shared Eve's ecstasy. The three other women of the chorus "daven" while the first woman describes the action. This davening is a rhythmic murmur like that of old women in churches and synagogues as they repeat and repeat familiar prayers and laments.

FIRST WOMAN OF THE CHORUS But Adam ate.
And Adam looked
At the creatures in the garden,
And at the ground
And at the wind and the water,
And he said: I am not the same as these.
And he began to examine
His skin and his eyes
And his ears and his nose and his mouth.
And he began to examine his own mind.
And he could not spit out the fruit
Nor swallow it.

Adam takes a second bite. All the actors, in a kind of ecstasy, form the serpent, moving in the same manner as we saw the serpent move with fewer actors earlier. The serpent, as played by all the actors, is still a display of the tree of life. It is seductive and inviting. Then the serpent separates.

A bag of apples is found on one side of the stage. An actor empties it out on the stage. The actors play with the apples, eat them and carry them out to the audience to share their pleasure with them.

THE CURSES

Adam begins to cough a little. It is clear that he can indeed neither swallow the fruit nor spit it out. Suddenly, an actor who has been playing one of the creatures in the garden pulls Adam up from under the arms. Adam himself speaks for God when God is speaking to Adam. When speaking for God, Adam uses a voice which is larger and more resonant than his usual one, and the actor who lifts him mouths the same words. Adam's own attitude, as he speaks for God, is one of surprise and dismay. Whenever God will speak, all the actors on stage will whisper his words too.

GOD (*speaking through Adam*)   Where are you?

The actor who had lifted Adam up now drops him and goes back to playing a creature in the garden. Adam tries to hide, and he tries to cough up the fruit to be able to speak clearly to God. But the fruit remains stuck in his throat. The same actor picks him up again.

GOD (*speaking through Adam*)   Where are you?
   Why do you not answer me?

The actor lets Adam drop and becomes a creature in the garden again.

ADAM (*answering God*)   I hear your voice in the garden
   And I am afraid.

Adam is picked up again. Whenever he is picked up to speak, his body goes limp.

142

GOD (*speaking through Adam*)   Before
   When you heard my voice
   You were not afraid,
   Yet, now you are afraid.

Adam is dropped again.

ADAM (*answering God*)   I am afraid
   Because I am naked
   And I have hidden myself.

Adam is picked up again from under the arms.

GOD (*speaking through Adam*)   Who told you.
   You were naked?
   Have you eaten of the tree
   From which
   I commanded you not to eat?

Adam is dropped.

ADAM (*answering*)   Lord, so long as I was alone
   I did not fall into sin.
   But as soon as this woman came,
   She tempted me.

Another actor now lifts up Eve in the same way Adam was lifted, and Eve is limp and speaks for God in a voice that is larger and more resonant than her usual one. The actor who lifts her, and the others, whisper the same words she is speaking.

GOD (*speaking through Eve*)   Woman, have you eaten of the tree
   Whereof I commanded you not to eat?

Eve is let drop, and the actor who had lifted her goes back to playing a creature in the garden.

EVE (*answering God*)   It was the serpent, Lord.
   He tempted me, and I ate.

SERPENT 1   You gave them a command,
   and I contradicted it.

SERPENT 2   Why did they obey me
   And not you?

From now on the voice of God is heard similarly through the different actors on the stage. All, except the four women of the chorus, lift each other in turn and speak with a voice that is larger than their usual ones. After lifting or being lifted, the actors return to being creatures in the garden. As the curses continue, there is a shorter space of time between them, and greater agitation in the garden. And as the curses are spoken, each by one actor, the other actors simultaneously whisper them to the audience.

GOD (*speaking through one actor who is lifted from under his arms by another actor*)   Because you have done this
   You are cursed over all animals.
   Upon your belly shall you go
   And dust shall you eat.

GOD (*speaking through another actor*)   Because you have eaten
   Of the tree of which I commanded you,
   Saying: You shall not eat of it,
   Cursed is the earth for your sake.

GOD (*speaking through another actor*)   You shall use your mind
   Not to understand but to doubt.
   And even if you understand,
   Still shall you doubt.

GOD (*speaking through another actor*)   When your children shall be
   found to murder,
   You shall make laws.
   But these laws shall not bind.

GOD (*speaking through another actor*)   You shall be made to think,
   And although few of your thoughts shall exalt you,
   Many of your thoughts shall bring you sorrow,
   And cause you to forget your exaltation.

GOD (*speaking through another actor*)   Now shall come a separation
   Between the dreams inside your head
   And those things which you believe

To be outside your head,
And the two shall war within you.

GOD (*speaking through another actor*)   Accursed, you shall be alone.
For whatever you think,
And whatever you see or hear,
You shall think it and see it and hear it, alone.
Henceforth shall you thirst after me.

GOD (*speaking through another actor*)   In the day shall you endure
The same longing as in the night,
And in the night shall you endure
The same longing as in the day.
Henceforth shall you thirst after me.

GOD (*speaking through another actor*)   And your children shall live in
fear of me.
And your children shall live in fear of you,
And your children shall live in fear of each other.

GOD (*speaking through another actor*)   Accursed, you shall glimpse
Eden
All the days of your life.
But you shall not come again.
And if you should come,
You would not know it.

GOD (*speaking through another actor*)   And in the end
The earth shall wax old like a garment
And be cast off by me.

GOD (*speaking through another actor*)   For that you were not able to
observe the command
Laid upon you, for more than one hour,
Accursed be your days.
Henceforth shall you thirst after me.

*With the volume increasing, the curses begin to overlap. They are repeated
and fragmented, spoken and whispered louder by an increasing number of
actors. Many actors are regularly picked up and dropped. It becomes*

increasingly impossible to distinguish whole phrases. All the voices build into a frenzy and a din of sound.

And in the day
Shall you endure the same longing
As in the night.

Henceforth shall you thirst after me.

And in the night
Shall you endure the same longing
As in the day.

Henceforth shall you thirst after me.

And now shall come a separation.

Accursed.

Between the dreams inside your head.

Accursed.

And those things which you believe to be outside your head,
And the two shall war within you.

And your children shall live in fear of me.

And in the end the earth shall wax old like a garment

And be cast off by me.

And your children shall live in fear of you.

You shall not come again to Eden.

And your children shall live in fear of each other.

And if you should come, you would not know it.

Accursed, you shall be made to think.

Accursed, you shall be alone.

And even when you understand,

Still shall you doubt.

Accursed.

Accursed.

Accursed.

Suddenly, there is silence. All the actors remain frozen a few seconds. Then Adam and Eve repeat, and continue to repeat throughout the next scene, their "locked" action of, respectively, accusing, and of reaching and subsiding.

STATEMENTS I

The four women are still kneeling.

FIRST WOMAN OF THE CHORUS   In the beginning anything is possible.

SECOND WOMAN OF THE CHORUS   I've lost the beginning.

THIRD WOMAN OF THE CHORUS   I'm in the middle.

FOURTH WOMAN OF THE CHORUS   Knowing neither the end nor the beginning.

Now they stand. They sway slightly from side to side.

FIRST WOMAN   One lemming.

SECOND WOMAN   One lemming.

THIRD WOMAN   One lemming.

FOURTH WOMAN   One lemming.

When they are not speaking their own statements, each of the women continues to say softly "one lemming" as an accompaniment to what the others are saying.

147

FIRST WOMAN I try sometimes to imagine
What it's like to be somebody else.
But it's always me pretending.
It has to be me.
Who else is there?

SECOND WOMAN I hugged my child
And sent him off to school
With his lunch in a paper bag.
And I wished he would never come home.

THIRD WOMAN I'm concerned
Because what you reject
Can still run your life.

FOURTH WOMAN I passed my friend on the street.

SECOND WOMAN I passed quite near.

FOURTH WOMAN I don't think she saw me.
If she did, I don't think

SECOND WOMAN She saw me see her.

FOURTH WOMAN I think she thought

SECOND WOMAN If she saw me—

FOURTH WOMAN That I didn't see her.

THIRD WOMAN If God exists,
It is through me.
And He will protect me
Because He owes His existence to me.

FIRST WOMAN Old stories have a secret.

SECOND WOMAN They are a prison.

THIRD WOMAN Someone is locked inside them.

FOURTH WOMAN Sometimes, when it's very quiet,
I can hear him breathing.

SECOND WOMAN   Sometimes I feel there's nothing to do
But help other people.
But as soon as I join a committee or a party,
I know that has nothing to do with it at all.

FOURTH WOMAN   Whatever I know—

SECOND WOMAN   I know it without words.

FOURTH WOMAN   I am here as a witness.

SECOND WOMAN   To what?

FOURTH WOMAN   I don't know.

THIRD WOMAN   It was different when I was a child.
I don't see any more bright colors.
There are no solid blocks
Or familiar rooms.

FIRST WOMAN   I went to a dinner.
The guests were pleasant.
We were poised,
Smiling over our plates,
Asking and answering the usual questions.
I wanted to throw the food,
Ax the table,
Scratch the women's faces,
And grab the men's balls.

SECOND WOMAN   When asked, I blamed it on the other person.
It wasn't me, I said.
It must have been her.
I could have said it was me,
But I said it was her.

THIRD WOMAN   My home was Cleveland.
Then I came to New York
And I didn't have to account to anybody.
I smoked: pot, hashish, opium.

I slept with a man.
I slept with a woman.
I slept with a man and a woman at the same time.
But I'm a gentle person, and I collapsed.

FOURTH WOMAN I'm still a child.

SECOND WOMAN So am I.

FOURTH WOMAN Sometimes people nod at you,
And smile,
And you know they haven't heard.

FIRST WOMAN On a certain day

SECOND WOMAN Of a certain year

THIRD WOMAN One lemming

FOURTH WOMAN Starts to run.

FIRST WOMAN Another lemming, seeing the first,

SECOND WOMAN Drops everything,

THIRD WOMAN And starts to run too.

FOURTH WOMAN Little by little

FIRST WOMAN All the lemmings

SECOND WOMAN From all over the country

THIRD WOMAN Run together

FOURTH WOMAN For tens

FIRST WOMAN And hundreds of miles

SECOND WOMAN Until,

FOURTH WOMAN Exhausted,

FIRST WOMAN They reach the cliff

SECOND WOMAN And throw themselves

THIRD WOMAN Into the sea.

CAIN AND ABEL

The four women continue to daven, but now without words, except when indicated. Davening-without-words is like a rhythmic humming, and it continues under the voices of the individual women who are speaking. Cain chops wood. Abel tends two sheep. The scene begins slowly to unfold between them. It will continue beyond the recital of the action by the chorus.

FOURTH WOMAN And when they were cast out
Eve and Adam remembered me.
And Eve conceived
And bore Cain,
And she said:

FOURTH AND SECOND WOMEN "Lo, I have gotten
A man from the Lord."

FOURTH WOMAN And again Adam and Eve remembered me.
And Eve bore Abel.
And again she said:

FOURTH AND SECOND WOMEN "Lo, I have gotten
A man from the Lord."

FOURTH WOMAN Then Eve had a dream,
And she ran and told it to Adam.
And Eve said,
"Lo, I saw Abel's blood flow from Cain's mouth."
And wishing to divert any evil that might come,
Adam separated Cain from Abel.
And Cain became a tiller of the ground,
And Abel a keeper of sheep.

And in time Cain offered unto the Lord
A sacrifice of first fruits,
While his brother Abel offered a firstborn lamb.
And the Lord had love for Abel and for his offering.
But for Cain and for his offering,
The Lord had no respect.
And Cain said:

FOURTH AND FIRST WOMEN   "Why did He accept your offering
And not mine?"

FOURTH WOMAN   And Cain's face grew dark,
And his words were not pleasing to the Lord.
And Cain said:

FOURTH AND FIRST WOMEN   "Why did He accept your offering
And not mine?"

FOURTH WOMAN   "There is no law
And there is no judge."
And the Lord spoke within him,
And He said:
"If you will amend your ways
I will forgive your anger.
Yet even now the power of evil
Crouches at the door."
But it occurred to Cain
That the world was created through goodness,
Yet he saw that good deeds bear no fruit.
And God said:
"It depends on you
Whether you shall be master over evil,
Or evil over you."
And Cain said:

FOURTH AND FIRST WOMEN   "Why did He accept your offering
And not mine?"

FOURTH WOMAN   And it occurred to Cain
That the world
Is ruled with an arbitrary power.
And Cain said:
"There is no law and there is no judge."

FOURTH AND FIRST WOMEN   "Else
Why did He not accept my offering,
Yet He accepted yours?"

FOURTH WOMAN   And it occurred to Cain
To kill his brother.
But it did not occur to Cain
That killing his brother
Would cause his brother's death.
For Cain did not know how to kill
And he struck at his brother.
And broke each of his bones in turn,
And this was the first murder.
And Cain said:
"If I were to spill your blood on the ground
As you do the sheep's,
Who is there to demand it of me?"
And Abel said:
"The Lord will demand it. The Lord will judge."
And Cain said:
"There is no judge. There is no law."

FOURTH AND FIRST WOMEN   "Else
Why did He accept your offering
And not accept mine?"

FOURTH WOMAN   "Why yours?
Why not mine?"
And it occurred to Cain
To kill his brother.
But it did not occur to Cain
That killing his brother

Would cause his brother's death.
For Cain did not know how to kill.
And he struck at his brother
And broke each of his bones in turn.
And Abel said: "The Lord will judge."
And Cain said: "There is no judge. There is no law."

FOURTH AND FIRST WOMEN   "Else
   Why did he accept your offering
   And not accept mine?"

FOURTH WOMAN   "Why yours?
   Why not mine?"
   And this was the first murder.
   For it occurred to Cain
   To kill his brother.
   But it did not occur to Cain
   That killing his brother
   Would cause his brother's death.

*Cain has come over to Abel. He feeds Abel's sheep, to get them out of his
way. He looks at Abel, and Abel looks back at Cain. The rest of the actors,
not including the chorus, breathe together regularly and quietly—they are
breathing Abel's breath. Cain tries different ways of killing Abel. After trying
each different way, he looks at Abel to see the result of what he has done, and
to try to decide what to do next. The rest of the company watches, and the
sheep remain quietly by. Some of the things that Cain does to Abel are to
pull at his limbs and to hold him in the air and contemplate dashing him on
the ground. Finally, he lays Abel down on the ground and, seeing that there
is still movement in the respiratory area, uses his hands to chop at Abel's
throat. Abel's breathing stops. All the sounds for hurting Abel and for the
chopping at him with his hands have come from the actor playing Cain, rather
than from the actor playing Abel. Now Cain listens for Abel's breathing,
which he misses hearing. He tries to breathe breath back into Abel from his
own mouth. Then he tries to stand Abel up. He puts grass into his lifeless
hand to try to have Abel feed the sheep. Finally, he lays Abel down on the
backs of his two sheep, standing behind him, swaying slightly from side to*

side, waiting, waiting for life to start up again in Abel. The heron from the garden is back, and it wanders near, making its gentle noise and standing on one leg and then the other. Cain continues to wait. The four women of the chorus make a small, long screeching sound from the backs of their throats. Abel, as a ghost, now crawls on his knees toward the front of the stage. He confronts the audience. The actor playing Abel is, at this moment, experiencing extreme tension throughout his body, and reseeing in his mind's eye what just happened to him. Cain, still watching the place where he put Abel's body on the sheep, continues to wait.

BLIND MEN'S HELL

The two actors who played the sheep, and one other actor, are on their backs on the floor. All the others, with the exception of the chorus, walk around and through them. All are blind and as if experiencing tremendous fatigue. They are like people who have lived too long. None of those who are walking may stop or fall—if they do, they must immediately get up and go on. Those on the floor grope upward, grabbing at parts of the moving people. This continues during Statements II.

STATEMENTS II

FIRST WOMAN OF THE CHORUS   In the beginning
　　Anything is possible.
　　From the center
　　I can choose to go anywhere.

SECOND WOMAN OF THE CHORUS   But now the point
　　Toward which I have chosen to go
　　Has a line drawn
　　Between itself
　　And the beginning.

FOURTH WOMAN OF THE CHORUS   I no longer know
  The beginning.
  I am in the middle.
  On a line
  Between the beginning
  And a point toward which I chose to go.

THIRD WOMAN OF THE CHORUS   I have fewer choices now.
  Because when I change my direction
  The change can only start
  From a line already drawn.

*Now the four women smile. They keep smiling unless they are speaking.
They sway slightly from side to side.*

SECOND WOMAN   I'm collecting things.
  Beads.
  I'm buying plants,
  Curtains—
  With which to make a home.
  I'm buying things
  To make a good life.

THIRD WOMAN   When I was thirteen
  I wanted a house of my own.
  The girl I was then
  Would say to me now:
  "What have you done with your advantages?
  You could have married a rich man,
  And had a big house.
  Instead, you're a freak."

FIRST WOMAN (*as the other women and she open and close one
  fist*)   Open.
  Close.
  Open.
  Close.
  No effort

Makes these two movements
One.

SECOND WOMAN   My husband is in that coffin.
In the day he goes to work.
In the evening we discuss household matters,
And at night
He climbs back into the coffin.

THIRD WOMAN   Even if you sit and do nothing,
Even so,
Your back is strapped to a wheel,
And the wheel turns.

FOURTH WOMAN   While we were in bed I asked a boy,

SECOND WOMAN   I asked him if he should be around—

FIRST WOMAN   If he should be around when I die,
Would he hold and rock me in his arms
For half an hour afterwards.

THIRD WOMAN   Because they can't tell.

FOURTH WOMAN   They can only approximate.

SECOND WOMAN   They can't tell when you're really dead.

FIRST WOMAN   Not exactly.

THIRD WOMAN   Not the exact moment.

SECOND WOMAN   When I was a child
This story was told to me in secret by a friend:
"A little boy came into his mother's room
And saw her naked.
'What's that?' he asked.
'It's a wound,' she said.
'What happened to your penis?' he asked.
'Oh,' she said,
'God chopped it off with an ax.'"

THIRD WOMAN (*with other women speaking and emphasizing the words "he," "his" and "him"*)   It's my husband.
He keeps me from it.
It's *his* fault.
He keeps me down, holds me at *his* level.
I could be happy
If it weren't for *him*.

FOURTH WOMAN   The doctors lie.
My mother died screaming with pain.
Did you know you could go into eternity
Screaming with pain?

FIRST WOMAN (*as the other women and she open and close one fist*)   Open.
Close.
Separate movements.
Stretched-out fingers.
Nails into skin.
One to open.
One to close.
Separate
Motions.
No matter how I try,
These movements
Are not one.
There is a stop between open
And close, and between close
And open.
No effort
Makes these two movements
One.
Close.
Open.
Close.

SECOND WOMAN   You can see them having lunch,

FIRST WOMAN Their faces pale,

THIRD WOMAN Laughing.
They are corpses laughing.

FOURTH WOMAN You can see them on the streets,

SECOND WOMAN Combed and brushed.

FIRST WOMAN They are colored pictures.

FIRST AND THIRD WOMEN The men have killed each other.

SECOND AND FOURTH WOMEN The King is dead.

FOURTH WOMAN He was shot in the head.

FIRST WOMAN By an unknown assassin.

SECOND WOMAN The men are dead.

THIRD WOMAN And no man can say
Of work or land:
"This is mine."

FIRST AND SECOND WOMEN The men are dead.

SECOND WOMAN We mourn them.

THIRD AND FOURTH WOMEN We are dead.

THIRD WOMAN We mourn ourselves.

FOURTH WOMAN If a bulldog ant
Is cut in two,
A battle starts
Between the head and the tail.
The head bites the tail.
The tail stings the head.
They fight
Until both halves are dead.

THIRD WOMAN So Man created God.
What for?
To set limits on himself.

FIRST WOMAN   Would my dreams recognize me?
Would they come to me and say
"She's the one who imagined us?"

THIRD WOMAN   I was queen over a country
Where the air was sweet.
We ate honey and fruit.
And at night
It was quiet.

SECOND WOMAN   Suddenly—
This moment.
Here, now.
I am here,
And you.
In this place, now
We are together.

FIRST WOMAN (*as the other three women, and finally she, begin to make the body sounds of the entering procession*)   At the very end.
Even after the end,
Even when the body is on its own,
The human being can make such a variety
Of sounds that it's amazing.
A field of dead men is loud.
Teeth clack, bones crack,
Limbs twist and drop,
And the last sound of all
Is a loud trumpet
Of escaping wind.

BEGATTING

Now all together the four women begin davening again, for a moment without words. The Blind Men's Hell has dissolved. Two actors, a man and a woman, begin very slowly approaching each other from either side of the stage. The four women are kneeling and rocking back and forth. All the others begin gently to explore each other's bodies.

THIRD WOMAN (*as the other three daven under her words*)   And Adam
Knew Eve and Eve knew Adam
And this was the first time.
And Adam knew Eve and Eve knew Adam
And this was the first time.

The actors are exploring each other's bodies as if for the first time. The women now open a book and read the "begats" from the Old Testament of the Bible. Each woman reads some part and then passes the book to another. But all are continually davening and, frequently, the exact words of the begatting are lost in favor of the rhythmic davening and the rocking back and forth toward the audience.

THIRD WOMAN (*reading*)   And Adam lived a hundred and thirty
years and he begat a son in his own likeness and he called his
name Seth.
    And the days of Adam after he had begotten Seth were eight
hundred years, and he begat sons and daughters.
    And Seth lived a hundred and five years and he begat Enos.
    And Seth lived after he begat Enos eight hundred and seven
years, and he begat sons and daughters.
    And Enos lived ninety years and he begat Cainan.
    And Enos lived after he begat Cainan eight hundred and
fifteen years, and he begat sons and daughters.
    And Cainan lived seventy years and begat Mahalaleel.

The man and woman come closer and closer to touching. The others have paired off, too, and are still exploring bodies.

FOURTH WOMAN (*reading*)   And Cainan lived, after he begat
Mahalaleel, eight hundred and forty years, and he begat sons and
daughters.
    And Mahalaleel lived sixty and five years, and he begat Jared.
    And Mahalaleel lived, after he begat Jared, eight hundred and
thirty years, and he begat sons and daughters.

And Jared lived a hundred and sixty and two years, and he begat Enoch.

And Jared lived after he begat Enoch eight hundred years, and he begat sons and daughters.

And Enoch lived sixty and five years and he begat Methuselah.

And Enoch walked with God after he begat Methuselah three hundred years, and he begat sons and daughters.

And Enoch walked with God and he was not, for God took him.

And Methuselah lived a hundred and eighty and seven years, and he begat Lamech.

And Methuselah lived after he begat Lamech seven hundred and eighty and two years, and he begat sons and daughters.

And Lamech lived a hundred and eighty and two years and he begat a son, and he called his name Noah.

And Lamech lived after he begat Noah five hundred and ninety years, and he begat sons and daughters.

And Noah was five hundred years old, and Noah begat Shem and Ham and Japheth.

By now, the two people have met in the center of the stage and embraced. All the couples are now exploring each other more gymnastically. They are trying to find how to make the connection between the male and the female body. They try various difficult positions. Eventually all make the connection and they copulate in increasingly faster rhythm.

FIRST WOMAN (*reading*)   And these are the generations of the sons of Noah and Shem and Ham and Japheth and the sons that were born to them after the flood:

The sons of Japheth were Gomer and Magog and Madai and Javan and Tubal and Meshech and Tiras.

And the sons of Gomer were Ashkenaz and Riphath and Togarmah.

And the sons of Javan were Elishah and Tarshish and Kittim and Dodanim.

And the sons of Ham were Cush and Mizraim and Phut and Canaan.

And the sons of Cush were Seba and Havilah and Sabtah and Raamah and Sabtechah.

And the sons of Raamah were Sheba and Dedan.

And Cush begat Nimrod, and he began to be a mighty one on earth.

And Canaan begat Sidon, his firstborn, and Heth.

And unto Shem were born Elam and Ashur and Arphaxad and Lud and Aram.

And the children of Aram were Uz and Hul and Gether and Mash.

And Arphaxad begat Salah, and Salah begat Eber.

And unto Eber were born two sons, and one was called Peleg, and his brother's name was Joktan.

And Joktan begat Almodad and Shelaph and Hazarmaveth and Jerah.

And Hadoram and Uzal and Dildah.

All the couples reach their climax at approximately the same time.
Immediately afterwards the women go into labor, and they then give birth.
Their sons are played by the actors who played their lovers. After the birth,
the mothers teach their children how to talk, walk, play games, etc.

SECOND WOMAN (*reading*)   And Obal and Abimael and Sheba, and Ophir and Havilah and Johab.

All these were the sons of Joktan.

And these were the generations of Shem.

Shem was a hundred years old and begat Arphaxad two years after the flood.

And Shem lived after he begat Arphaxad five hundred years, and he begat sons and daughters.

And Arphaxad lived five and thirty years and he begat Salah.

And Arphaxad lived after he begat Salah four hundred and three years, and he begat sons and daughters.

And Salah lived thirty years and he begat Eber.

And Salah lived after he begat Eber four hundred and three years, and he begat sons and daughters.

And Eber lived four hundred and thirty years and he begat Peleg.

And Eber lived after he begat Peleg four hundred and thirty years, and he begat sons and daughters.

And Peleg lived thirty years and he begat Reu.

And Peleg lived after he begat Reu two hundred and nine years, and he begat sons and daughters.

And Reu lived thirty and two years, and he begat Serug.

And Reu lived after he begat Serug two hundred and seven years, and he begat sons and daughters.

And Serug lived thirty years and he begat Nahor.

And Serug lived after he begat Nahor two hundred years, and he begat sons and daughters.

And Nahor lived twenty and nine years, and he begat Terah.

And Nahor lived after he begat Terah a hundred and nineteen years, and he begat sons and daughters.

And Terah lived seventy years, and he begat Abram and Nahor and Haran.

And these are the generations of Terah.

From being small children, the men of the company have become very old people. They are brought forward, helped slowly, to the front of the stage by their mothers, who have remained young. One or two of the actresses play old women and also stay at the front of the stage.

THIRD WOMAN (*reading*)   Terah begat Isaac, and Isaac begat Jacob, and Jacob begat Judah and his brethren.

And Judah begat Phares and Zarah, of Thainar.

And Phares begat Esrom.

And Esrom begat Aram.

And Aram begat Aminadab.

And Aminadab begat Naasson.

And Naasson begat Salmon.

And Salmon begat Booz, of Rachab.

And Booz begat Obed, of Ruth.

And Obed begat Jesse.

And Jesse begat David the King.

And David the King begat Solomon, of her that had been the wife of Urias.

And Solomon begat Rehoboam.

And Rehoboam begat Abia.

And Abia begat Asa.

And Asa begat Josaphat.

And Josaphat begat Joram.

And Joram begat Ozias.

And Ozias begat Joatham.

And Joatham begat Achaz.

And Achaz begat Ezekias.

And Ezekias begat Manasses.

And Manasses begat Amon.

And Amon begat Josias.

And Josias begat Jechonias and his brethren about the time they were carried away to Babylon.

And after they were brought to Babylon, Jechonias begat Salathiel.

And Salathiel begat Zorobabel.

And Zorobabel begat Abiud.

And Abiud begat Eliakim.

And Eliakim begat Azor.

And Azor begat Sadoc.

And Sadoc begat Achim.

And Achim begat Eliud.

And Eliud begat Eleazur.

And Eleazur begat Mathan.

And Mathan begat Jacob.

And Jacob begat Joseph.

OLD PEOPLE

There is now a line of old people facing the audience at the front of the stage. They speak out a name or two, or mumble, from the many names of the "begatting." The four women of the chorus are davening without words. The other actresses, the ones who have just played the mothers, are at the back of the stage, and they daven, too, softly.

THE SONG

The actors move about freely on the stage. Each is overtaken by a slow kind of dying, not so much a physical one as a kind of "emptying out," a living death, which soon slows them to a complete stop. Each actor has a final small physical tremor. Then, as if ghosts, the actors begin to sing a sentimental popular song from twenty or thirty years ago. No longer as ghosts but as themselves they continue singing the song as they leave the theater, walking out through the audience.

EAT CAKE

photo courtesy of Michael Smith

Eat Cake premiered in August 1971 at The Changing Scene in Denver, directed by Michael Smith.

A middle-class American room: much furniture, many appliances, gadgets and conveniences—as if the room were a magazine ad for a department store. Nancy, the woman of the house, is pretty. Wearing a black nylon slip, she admires her hair in the mirror. She is pleased that her hair looks as well dyed and combed as hair in a shampoo commercial. Although we cannot see the monitor, we can hear Nancy's television set. A pleasing male voice seems to address Nancy personally. As she hears the voice, Nancy continues to admire herself in the mirror, posing prettily now with her vacuum cleaner.

MAN'S VOICE Stop. Take it easy. Relax a while. You're beautiful, you're young. Your husband earns well. You have pretty children. Look in the mirror. You're pretty as a picture.

Overly sweet background music plays behind the voice. This music will continue throughout the play.

You're one of the very lucky. Your skin is creamed, your hair is styled, you wear the latest. No product in the world is too good for you. You are an American. You may use your husband's credit card to vacation anywhere in the world. You may have two, even three children and keep your figure. You bend gracefully when you empty the garbage pail wearing white gloves and not getting a spot on them. You may smoke, wash dishes in your dishwasher, read magazines, go out in a new frock, eat the best available packaged cereal. Every morning in full view of your neighbors, you may kiss your husband lightly on the cheek as he goes to work. You may buy dinnerware and flatware, tablecloths, place mats, sheets, rugs, garden hoses, shoe trees, cultured pearls and any number of stockings. You are as royal as the woman in the White House. You are one of the nicest girls in the world, and the luckiest, and the prettiest . . .

Nancy continues looking at herself in the mirror, cupping her breasts lightly, pouting a little, assuming poses, tossing her hair, completely playing the game of being the lovable object—being like the models and actresses she has seen on television. As the voice on television fades down and the television music fades up, Nancy vacuums in a dreamy way. Behind her we see a man slip into the house. He is neat and attractive, dressed in burglar

169

black. He stands for a moment looking at Nancy. He might be a fantasy of hers, a man who has stepped off the TV screen. He might also be a young executive indulging in a perverse little hobby. From behind her he puts his hands over her eyes. She screams a ladylike little scream.

NANCY   Oh! Who is it? Is it you, Charlie? Is it Charlie the milkman playing a little game with me? Answer me! The milkman? Is it the milkman? (*Not certain what TV show she might be on, she tries to find the appropriate way to act. For the moment she decides this is not a comedy but a drama, so she tries to break away.*) Whoever you are, I am going to pierce you with my fingernails. I am not as helpless as I look.

He allows her to break away. Everything she does seems to amuse him mildly, as if he were watching the antics of a child.

What do you want? What show are we on? Do you want me to answer some questions?

He shakes his head no.

Are you sure? Have I won something?

He smiles, shakes his head no.

I'm on camera, aren't I? I am. I know I am. I am.

He shakes his head no. She changes her tack.

Are you a salesman? Are you selling?

He shakes his head no.

I only buy when I'm in the mood. I'm not in the mood. As a matter of fact, I have a slight headache. (*She looks at him hopefully.*) Doctor? I haven't been feeling entirely well. I have a slight pain down here. (*She indicates her lower back.*) I'm sure it's nothing serious. But if you'd like to touch, Dr. Harlowe . . .

He's apparently not into this game either.

You're not "Dr. Harlowe and the Nurses"? Well, who are you?

(She's getting exasperated.) Do you sing or something? *(She waits to see if he will start to sing. He doesn't. She drops her poses, puts her hands on her hips and faces him square on.)* Well what *do* you want?

When the man speaks we recognize his soft sexy voice as the voice on Nancy's TV.

MAN   Take your clothes off.

NANCY   Why should I?

MAN   Because I'm a rapist.

NANCY   Oh, I'm going to scream.

MAN *(calm but meaning it)*   Don't or I'll strangle you.

NANCY *(remembering something she has seen on TV)*   I see. You just stay calm now. I want to be your friend.

MAN   Good. Take your clothes off.

NANCY   Okay.

She takes off her clothes in a slow provocative manner. When she reaches her panties she is really getting into it, but he stops her.

MAN   That's enough.

NANCY   Enough?

MAN   Get a bathrobe. Your most attractive bathrobe. Put it on.

NANCY   Oh. *(She rushes to get a bathrobe, puts it on, arranges it fetchingly, smiling at him as if she were in a lingerie ad.)*

MAN   Run your fingers through your hair.

She does. This is something she knows how to do.

   Comb it out.

She does this too, glamorously.

NANCY   Is this how you get your kicks?

MAN No, there's one other thing.

NANCY What's that?

MAN Open the refrigerator.

She goes to the refrigerator, opens it.

NANCY You *are* selling something.

MAN Stand there.

She poses for him.

Very nice. Now look inside.

She bends over to look inside, tilting up her rear end, supposing this is what he wants.

Is there any cake?

NANCY Any what?

MAN Is there any cake in the refrigerator?

NANCY There's some left over from yesterday.

MAN Bring it to the table.

NANCY (*doing so*) Yes?

MAN Now sit and eat it.

NANCY Eat it? That's a big piece of cake.

MAN Eat it.

NANCY I'm on a diet.

MAN Eat it.

NANCY I know. There's a prize in it, isn't there? A surprise prize—I can't wait.

She eats the cake, expecting to bite on a prize. He watches. She finishes eating. She's disappointed.

Nothing. There's no prize?

With a towel, he carefully wipes cake off her face as he would a baby's.

MAN (*holding Nancy's phone*)   All right now. I'm going to dial a number.

NANCY (*pleased*)   Yes? So this *is* a game. Goody.

MAN   There is a bake shop three blocks from here. They deliver. I want you to order three large birthday cakes. You understand? Insist they bring them over now. Then place a standing order for one cake in the morning, one in the evening, and one at noon— every day this coming week. You have that?

She nods dumbly. He hands her the phone. She stares at him dumbfounded. He motions her to speak to the bakery.

NANCY   Hello? Hello. This is Nancy Garrison, thirty-five Alpine—thirty-five. I need three large birthday cakes for tonight. I mean for now—as soon as possible. What do you mean, you can't? I need them now. Yes, now—or I don't want them at all. I need them *immediately.*

She is getting into it. He smiles at her encouragingly.

The largest one you have. Nancy. "Happy Birthday, Nancy." I'm having a surprise birthday party. Yes, for myself. I'll pay you on delivery.

He whispers to her what to say next. She plays along.

In fact I also want to place a standing order for one birthday cake in the morning, one at noon, and one in the evening every day this week. It's, uh, a mothers' get-together. All the children in the school are having birthdays this week and I, uh, bring the cake.

He whispers to her again.

Would you put some brownies in too, in the mornings, say a dozen? And cupcakes in the evening with the evening order?

Chocolate—no, mixed. Yes. Yes, that's right. . . . Every morning and every night, that's right. Brownies and cake in the morning. Cupcakes and cake in the evening. Yes, I promise to pay on delivery. What? Pink—pink and yellow. (*She hangs up.*)

MAN (*immediately*)   Other bakeries.

NANCY   I don't know the numbers of bakeries.

MAN   Get the directory.

She does while he clears the table and neatly wipes it down.

Now at each bakery you're to vary the order. Cookies instead of brownies with the cake in the morning. Chocolates or macaroons with the cake at noon. Éclairs or cream puffs, whichever you want, with the cake at night. And better make them all birthday cakes. "Happy Birthday, Nancy" is very good. Order them all as birthday cakes to yourself.

NANCY   They'll think I'm crazy.

MAN   Tell them you're running a nationwide club of women whose name is Nancy and have a birthday this week. They subscribe at the beginning of the year, then when it's birthday time a cake arrives with their name on it, plus sweets: Nancy's Surprise Birthday Cake Club for Women Named Nancy.

NANCY   Listen, I don't have more than twenty-five dollars in my purse.

MAN   That'll do for today. Tomorrow I'll go with you to the bank.

NANCY   Tomorrow?

MAN   I'm taking up residence here.

NANCY   Here? Where?

MAN   In that closet, to be exact. If you try to tell anyone about me I'll come out of the closet and kill you. You're to find an excuse to keep your family away, and at the end of the week I'll leave. Now get on the phone and place the order.

NANCY   I'm going to scream.

He slaps her lightly across the face.

NANCY (*quieting nicely, just as she has seen hysterical women do on soaps*) Oh.

She dials. The lights fade. We hear her voice ordering on the phone.

NANCY'S VOICE   Nancy. That's right. "Happy Birthday, Nancy." Chocolate layer. I don't care what color frosting. Sorry, wait. I do—pink and yellow. On all of them? Yes. With a dozen brownies in the morning, six napoleons at noon. Nancy Garrison. I'm running a private club for women named Nancy having a birthday. Whipped cream puffs with cake at night. Éclairs, cream puffs and almond dreams. Thank you very much. Hello, Walter's Bakery, this is Nancy Garrison, thirty-five Alpine. Yes, three times a day. With macaroons in the mornings. With a quart—no, two quarts of ice cream at noon. I don't care—wait. Butternut swirl. With the cake at night please two pounds cookies. Chocolate chip. Yes, I'll pay on delivery. No, I don't want to open a charge account. Thank you. Brownies, fudge—half a pound. Six prune Danish. Thank you very much. Chocolate layer. Pink and yellow. "Happy Birthday, Nancy." Cream puffs. Éclairs. Cookies: chocolate chip. Two quarts ice cream—butternut swirl . . .

As the lights come up we see there are empty cake cartons all over the room. Nancy is eating cake. She has gotten a little fat. Three cakes sit on the table in front of her, ready to be eaten. The man sits in a chair, watching her with interest.

MAN   Eat.

NANCY   I can't.

MAN   You're three cakes behind schedule.

NANCY   I'm going to be sick.

MAN   I won't allow you to vomit until halfway through the second cake. I told you that. After vomiting you eat the next cake and a half.

NANCY   Please.

MAN   (*relenting*)   If you like you can save the brownies until the middle of the afternoon to eat with the cream puffs.

NANCY   Are you enjoying this?

MAN   Yes.

NANCY   Why?

MAN   I don't know.

NANCY   Are you being paid?

MAN   Eat. Don't try to distract me.

NANCY   Could we make a little deal, maybe?

MAN   I can have all the sex I want outside.

NANCY   But I'm fond of you.

MAN   That's *your* hang-up. I'm a rapist.

The doorbell rings. Nancy goes to answer it, the man keeping an eye on her.

NANCY'S VOICE FROM OFFSTAGE   Thank you very much.

Nancy returns with three more cake cartons.

MAN   You're six cakes behind schedule.

NANCY   What if I stop?

MAN   Eat.

Without a fork, she stuffs the cake into her mouth fast. The doorbell rings again. She rushes toward the door. He catches her and twists her arm behind her back.

If you start to say anything I will kill you from the back. Is that clear?

She nods, goes to the door and comes back with parcels.

Unwrap.

She unwraps the cake.

Inscription?

NANCY *(reading)*   "Happy Birthday, Nancy."

MAN   Frosting?

NANCY *(looking)*   The usual. Yellow with pink things.

MAN   Inside?

She plunges her hand directly into the cake and pulls out its insides.

NANCY   Chocolate layer.

MAN   Eat.

She stuffs cake into her mouth.

Next. Inscription?

She opens another cake carton.

NANCY   "Happy Birthday, Nancy."

MAN   Frosting?

NANCY   Yellow with pink things.

MAN   Inside?

NANCY *(plunging her hand in, pulling out the inside of the cake)*   Chocolate layer.

MAN   Eat.

She tries to stuff the whole cake into her mouth. What cake lands on the floor he picks up and starts to push into her mouth. The lights go down. In the dark we hear the magnified sounds of Nancy's eating, burping and vomiting, accompanied by soap opera music. The lights come up dimly. Nancy, looking fat, is lying on the couch eating. Cake cartons surround her. We see the shadow of the man, looking very tall, high above Nancy operating a huge pastry froster, jerking down giant gobs of frosting on her.

MAN'S VOICE *(calmly)*   Eat. Eat. Eat.

The lights come back up to normal. Nancy is still on the couch, eating. Her face, her clothes and the couch are smeared with cake. Only the man, standing near Nancy, remains immaculately clean.

MAN *(gently)*   This is the last day. You've done very well. Eat.

Nancy eats mechanically. Unseen by her, the man slips out the door. His voice comes from the television.

MAN'S VOICE   You're one of the lucky. Your skin is creamed, your hair is styled, you wear the latest fashions. No product made anywhere in the world is too good for you. You are American. You are free. You are one of the nicest girls in the world, one of the prettiest, one of the nicest—

Suddenly there is no more sound from the television. Nancy, startled by the silence, looks up from her eating. Slowly she realizes she is alone. The full horror of what has happened dawns on her.

NANCY *(screaming)*   Rape! RAPE! RAPE!!!

BAG LADY

Shami Chaikin in *Bag Lady*

photo by Gerry Vezzuso

Bag Lady premiered in November, 1979 in New York at the Theater for the New City. It featured Shami Chaikin and was directed by Elinor Renfield, with costumes by Mary Brecht and music by Peter Golub. In 1981 *Bag Lady,* with Shami Chaikin and directed by Steve Kent, played off-Broadway at the Manhattan Theater Club as part of an evening of three van Itallie plays.

Bag Lady *takes place on the streets of New York City, which Clara, born in pre-Holocaust Europe, calls home. Clara goes about her business, stuffing her shopping bags with assorted oddments. When she feels assailed by voices of passersby, she responds humorously and belligerently. She ruminates on past and present, proclaiming her sovereignty as the quintessential urbanite. She's like the city itself, with all its terrors. Sometimes, like a crazy Zen monk, she imagines the nuclear end of New York.*

It's a late November afternoon. An empty bench in a tiny New York park is surrounded by a chain-link fence. Near the bench lurk two or three big dangerous-looking shards of black plastic refuse. We hear the voices of people passing on the street a few feet away.

GIRL'S VOICE   How about a frozen yogurt?

BOY'S VOICE   No.

GIRL'S VOICE   It's all natural.

BOY'S VOICE   Too cold.

GIRL'S VOICE   Jesus.

During the next set of voices we overhear from the street, Clara enters the park through a gash in the fence. Clara's in her early fifties, probably. She wears a big man's overcoat. She carries her bags and a walking stick. She mutters to herself.

VOICE OF FIRST PERSON   I *said* never mind.

VOICE OF SECOND PERSON   But you haven't accepted it emotionally.

VOICE OF FIRST PERSON (*speaking fast*)   Yes I have.

VOICE OF SECOND PERSON   Do you want me to feel guilty?

VOICE OF FIRST PERSON   Forget it.

VOICE OF SECOND PERSON   All I said was, "Do you want to go to the Chinese restaurant?" Nothing's ever easy with you, is it?

VOICE OF FIRST PERSON   Okay. So where do *you* want to eat?

VOICE OF SECOND PERSON We could have Chinese food. I don't care.

VOICE OF FIRST PERSON Whatever you say.

Street voices and noises die down. Throughout the play, however, we will hear the sounds of the street mixed with the music in Clara's mind. Clara sometimes hears a clock ticking in her head.

CLARA *(muttering, placing her stick carefully by her)* Okay . . . You never know . . . Inspect the damages . . . Okay . . . travel light . . . the discard bag, that's it . . . travel light . . .

Clara has settled herself on the ground, with the bench behind her for protection. Tired, she rests a moment. She is surrounded by her bags. Her bags contain all she owns. She knows what's inside them as well as any home owner knows her closets. Believing one bag was broken into, Clara needs time in this relatively secure park to inspect the ravages. She also needs to lighten her load, to travel more lightly. She must decide what to keep, what to discard. She sets up one bag as a discard bag. She puts the contents of another bag on the ground. We hear noises from the nearby playground. Clara finds a clock in her stuff. She calls out to a passerby whom we don't see.

What time is it? *(She goes back to her bags.)* I never seem to have a clock that works. Who cares? Sometimes it's now, sometimes it's five minutes ago . . . *(She looks worried; five minutes ago was when she believes her bag was vandalized.)* Sometimes its twenty years from now when the city will be over. *(She can easily picture this in her mind.)* Who cares? *(She is re-sorting, laying out her things one by one.)* Only essentials. White tablecloth. My clock. Brandy. The flowered teapot. *(She hesitates over the flowered teapot.)* Got to go. *(Sighing, she reluctantly places it in the discard pile. But then she fishes it out again and places it on the bench behind her with the things she really cares about. She is creating a little altar of objects there. She checks her little bag of essentials.)* Only essentials. My little bag. The Marseilles pictures.

She lays out the pictures—which are not real photographs but objects or magazine pictures she has found, wrapped carefully and saved, attributing to each a personal meaning. She speaks conversationally to the audience, as if we were a friend.

I have a piece of velvet here I want to show you. You wouldn't happen to have a bottle on you, would you? Brandy? I love velvet and old silk. Old silk and satin. I like sequins and tassels and all that trash too. Would you believe I'm a virgin? I am. A man tried to rape me once. New Brunswick, New Jersey. Can't stand the suburbs. (*She puts on a sequined sweater that has fallen from a bag.*) But he didn't touch me. Not the Virgin Queen. (*She shows us a picture.*) I was eleven. Marseilles, France. That's Mama. (*She examines Mama.*) She always looked old. (*Mama's picture goes with the essentials. She puts another piece of clothing on over the sweater.*) I like to have on just the right thing—you know, for the season, for the occasion. Would you do me a favor? I'd like an orange Crush. You know how you get a craving? Get one for yourself too. These are my winter boots. And this is my fur. It's sable or fox or something. (*She puts on and caresses a ratty old fur piece.*) You have to own everywhere you go, you know: your own furs, your own house, your own yacht. Otherwise you have to go to welfare hotels and they take your things and send you to the camps. (*She picks out a red sweater.*) This was Jackie's. I picked it up from her pile on Fifth Avenue. It has a moth hole. She doesn't bother fixing things—just throws them out. Like me. (*Jackie's sweater is tossed onto the discard pile.*) I saw her get into a cab once. She likes cashmere. (*She retrieves the sweater from the discard pile.*) So do I. We like sitting around in it. There's millions rushing, so why not just sit around? I know a woman with cancer was cured just by sitting still. Why not? Know how many people have cancer now? Everybody. I know a woman on the subway used to shout at people to stop smoking 'cause she was getting lung cancer. I don't know if they still smoke on the subway. I never take the subway. (*She shows another picture.*) My aunt Lara who took care of me while her daughters Lisa and Rose worked in the dress factory with Mama. That's Uncle Max in his waiter's uniform. He wasn't supposed to work in a restaurant. He had no papers.

That's why they took him away. They took Mama and Lara and Rose too. They weren't supposed to be working anywhere either. They weren't smart like me. I don't work. (*She gets up and sits on the bench.*) I just sit around. I'm smart. I'm really a singer. A few years ago I made all those Judy Garland albums. That was my voice they used. (*She sings while applying powder from a compact.*) "I'll get by as long as I have you . . ." I wasn't a star right away of course. I had to be discovered first. But then I had breakfast in bed and the maid said, "Good morning, Miss Elizabeth." (*She is applying lipstick.*) I was playing Elizabeth Taylor. I had a big house right across the street from the studio. You can stay there if you're ever in L.A.; I'll lend you the key. Once when I walked across the street to the studio I found someone playing my very own part of Judy Garland. You can't trust people out there. But don't get me wrong: I love Hollywood. (*She sings.*) "There's no business like show business." I played Queen Elizabeth in the movies, my Bette Davis part. You feel like a hamburger? I do. A lot of men want me 'cause I'm a wealthy woman. But do I want them? Ugh. Do you like my hair pulled back this way? (*She plays the coquette in a clownish way. Her hair is actually pulled back by a red sweater band throughout the play.*) This is how they used to do it at the studio every morning at five. Then they'd pull me in with one of those waist pullers. (*She pulls in her stomach and her cheeks, pulls her hair back.*) And they dyed my hair blonde. Queen Elizabeth has guards when she walks in the street. I don't need them. Nobody dares talk to me unless I talk to them first. Ever notice? It's protocol. I'm the Empress. My brother's the King of Moscow. (*For a crown she puts on an old hat.*) Poor Tsar. Poor Papa. Papa knew it was coming. You can tell from his face. Look. (*She shows us a photo of the assassinated Russian royal family.*) But what was he supposed to say? There we all were cooped up in this tiny room—nothing like the castles we were used to—and we played gin rummy like nothing was wrong. Papa said everything was okay. Only Anastasia escaped. Of course wherever she is, she's had to change her name. (*broad wink*) *Ponyimayish?* (*sitting*

on the bench, holding her stick, becoming quite grand) I went to visit
the Shah once in Persia. He was staying by the seashore in a big
hotel, the Fontainebleau. There was a pool up there on the roof
and his wife was swimming. "Come on in, Clara. Don't be
scared—the water's fine." She was pretty, but I liked looking at
him. He looked like the Tsar—the beard, the moustache—so
handsome. My brother was the Tsar's assistant. He's in Moscow
now but I've lost his address. You haven't seen my little leather
address book, have you? With the little gold pencil? I should
really write to *Monsieur* Morganstern—if I had his address . . .
When the train was leaving Marseilles *Monsieur* Morganstern
said, "Don't forget to write, Clara." *Cher Monsieur* Morganstern,
How are you? Is everything all right in Marseilles now the war's
over? I'm fine. I'm the Empress of New York. Only essentials.
(*Stately with her stick, she walks, reviewing her belongings from on
high. Then, her interest caught by a yellow swatch of cloth, she sits on
the ground to examine it.*) Yellow swatch: fabric for the chairs in
the dining room in Hollywood. Okay. (*She saves that.*) Lipstick.
My Jackie sweater. Timetable: planes to Moscow. Blue purse.
Keys. Palm Beach phone book. Phone number of the yacht.
Want it? You can tell the captain I said it's okay. Robert
Kennedy cushion, or bag—depending. Okay. Potato chips.
Matches. Toilet paper purse. White tablecloth. Rubber bands.
Sunglasses. Extra brandy bottle. The cotton in the blue box.
Letter to my brother, the King of Moscow—unfinished. This
city is going to be a museum someday after it stops. This'll all be
valuable. Piece of lace to make a collar. Silk undies. Silk keeps
you warm, you know. My pink slippers with the pom-poms.
My Russian blouse with the flowers. Chuckles for before
sleeping. Extra toilet paper. The feather. Argyle socks. Alarm
clock. The Mickey Mouse wristwatch. The yacht and the house
in L.A., fine—but with me, only what I can carry. That's my
rule. I move for the winter around the corner here to where it's
warm in front of the dry cleaner's. How about picking me up a
jar of peanut butter? Sometimes I get this craving for peanut
butter, but I can't leave my post right now. People are used to

seeing me here. Don't worry about a spoon—I can use my fingers. It's wartime, you know. It's not wartime? Sorry, I was misinformed. There's one of my regulars—she brings me coffee every morning in a mug and puts it down here. I threw out my Fiestaware. You gotta let things go. Throw them out. Move on. Nothing extra. That way you can move right out of the city when there's a war, move for the winter to Florida, be ready for anything.

Siren sound from the street. The sounds from the playground are louder.

It's my choice. Ladies don't go to the welfare hotel. They rape you, that's why. At the Women's Home they're a bunch of old ladies. No drinking, no smoking and if you talk back, like Nazis they send you to Bellevue. At Bellevue it's a toss-up. Either they keep you one night and you're out, or they send you to the killing place where they kill you with drugs in a month unless you escape. That's why I live here. Safer. And when I want, I go to Florida. 'Course there's a lot of bums from New York down there so I have my yacht. Nobody comes on board unless I want them to. I tell the captain: head out to sea and don't turn around till I tell you. I sit on deck and watch the stars . . . you know. I like just sitting around. How about getting me a brandy there at the liquor store? Say it's for me. They know me. Tell 'em the Empress wants her brandy.

She is going through her things more rapidly, trying to find something. The street sounds are more present. It's getting darker, as it is closer to sunset.

This whole city's a hospital. I see 'em go by. Everybody's a patient. Tit cancer. Heart attack. Ass cancer. Everybody's rushing to the hospital. I've got a subway map right here— only I never take the subway. (*She screams out to a passerby.*) So forget it! Anybody want a subway map? (*Immediately, realizing she might be arrested for causing a commotion, she claps her hand over her mouth. She talks to herself, quieting herself like a mother would a child.*) No, don't look at them. Sit down. Smile. Shut up. Be a good quiet crazy. Smile. Shut up. (*Suddenly Clara feels an itch. To*

scratch she has to work her way through layers of clothing.) Itch.
Scratch. Pass your hand under the elastic band, past the flannel,
past the slip, under it to the skin and then—scratch. Can't. The
white chemise is in the way. Scratch a hole through it. Your
pretty white chemise? Yeah, well, it's an itch. In case of
emergency—scratch. Can't. Why not? It's not cotton—just some
cheap nylon. Get the nail file, cut a slit. Emergency. Skin calling.
Itch. Got to scratch. Nail file, nail file? In the blue plastic sewing
kit, "Souvenir of Gainesville, Florida." Well, get it. And don't
drop your white tablecloth on the sidewalk, asshole, it's linen.
Never mind. Got to scratch. Emergency. Try the other bag.
Can't with one hand. Drop the chemise. Don't want to. Itch.
Use the toothpick. Push the toothpick through the chemise.
Toothpick . . . toothpick? In the red-check napkin around the
piece of rye. Got it! Repack. Now. But the itch . . . Repack!
Now! Can't have your stuff all over everywhere. But—
emergency—itch—might be a louse. Shit. Delousing at that
shitty shelter. Got to scratch. Shit, shit, shit.

We hear the voices of two men passing by.

FIRST MAN'S VOICE   Those guys are the fucking pricks of the
world, man. The Russians have the Middle East by the balls.
Listen, do you still want to go to the copy place?

SECOND MAN'S VOICE   Sure, but after. It's no use schlepping all
that stuff to the gym. It won't fit in the locker.

We hear the voices of two women passing by.

FIRST WOMAN'S VOICE   So . . . that's it. That's my story.

SECOND WOMAN'S VOICE   Fantastic. Great.

FIRST WOMAN'S VOICE   Yeah.

SECOND WOMAN'S VOICE   I mean that's fabulous.

FIRST WOMAN'S VOICE   I know.

SECOND WOMAN'S VOICE   You've really gotten your life together.

FIRST WOMAN'S VOICE Thanks.

SECOND WOMAN'S VOICE So—what else do you want me to say?

We are more aware of street sounds. It is getting darker. More anxious, Clara addresses people on the street.

CLARA Would you believe I'm a virgin? I am. Can't stand the suburbs. Fuck you, Japetto. (*Now she talks to us.*) What's clumsy about me? Everything. Wipe. (*She puts order in her bags. She holds up an object.*) It's an Easter egg. Pretty, isn't it? Gold and red . . . And on the inside it's rotten and it smells. (*She laughs harshly, addresses another person passing by.*) Hey, Mr. Rich and Handsome, how 'bout buying an old girl a drink? (*She goes back to the pictures.*) This is Papa. Papa was handsome, Mama said. Papa was a baker. In Minsk. Uncle Max wrote how wonderful it was in Marseilles. He was a liar, Uncle Max. So Mama and Papa took the train to Marseilles. Only Papa had a heart attack on the train and Mama got to Marseilles pregnant with me. This is my half brother. He stayed in Russia. He's the King of Moscow. I've lost his address. He'd take care of me if he knew where I was. (*She shouts to someone passing.*) Egg salad sandwich. Hey, missus, would you, please? An egg salad sandwich? You want one? We could have one together. No time? Well, sorry. That's life. Hey, don't mean to impose. I know I take up a lot of room. Queens do. Hello. Good-bye. No need to stand on ceremony. I'm not your family. Just friends. Hey, mister, you look like a nice boy. You want to run over to McDonald's for me?

Voices of a woman and a man passing on the street.

WOMAN'S VOICE I think we're feeling the same thing. We're just calling it by different names.

MAN'S VOICE Okay, so analyze it, go ahead.

WOMAN'S VOICE I can't when you have that petulant sound in your voice.

MAN'S VOICE Don't give me that crap again. Shit.

CLARA   Oh, well. Well, Clara dear, I'd like to tell you a little story. Once upon a time not here, something happened. Between black plagues and before everyone died young. Did it happen to the Empress? Well, maybe it didn't happen there. Maybe it was in that Hallmark card in the snow. Wouldn't that be nice? Your favorite, Clara, where is it? (*She goes digging in a bag.*) The house in the snow at Christmas with the gold sprinkles . . . (*She looks without finding it.*) Here come those two guys again—the small one with the long white scarf like Rita Hayworth and the big one in the leather jacket.

From the street we hear a man's voice.

MAN'S VOICE   I *know* I don't say it very often. It's not my style. But once and for all I love you. Okay? Is everything okay now?

CLARA   The big one just keeps crying and crying. But Rita Hayworth won't give him the time of day. He hurts, the big one hurts—but Rita won't even look at him. How do you like that?

From the street we hear the voice of an angry mother.

VOICE OF ANGRY MOTHER   Get over here, you little monster, or I'll crack your head open!

CLARA   (*looking at someone else's legs*)   Look, look at her shoes! How'd you learn to walk on those icicle heels, lady, at circus school? (*She looks at her clock.*) Busted. Past mending. All gone. Still, I'll keep it. Never can tell. Like my hat? The feather? Like it? No? Too bad. Isn't she funny? All day long. Questions. Answers. Repeats. Takes a bow. Just like a real Pinocchio. I'm Pipipipipinocchio! I can sing. I can dance. "I got rhythm, I got rhythm." Just like every other little American girl—or almost. Hey, Japetto, how 'bout an American quarter for an all-American girl? Oh, thank, you. Thank you, Japetto. (*She picks up a coin that was tossed to her, puts it down her bosom. Then, when the donor is out of earshot . . .*) Fuck you, Japetto. Thank you, Japetto. Fuck you, Japetto. Exciting. Keep going. You're doing fine, Clara. Where were we? "Miss Elizabeth Taylor?" Yes. "One moment, please. Marseilles calling." No. Wipe. (*She sits back on the bench.*) "You're such a good girl, Clara." Mama! No. Wipe. Stomach. That's the ticket. It's your stomach calling, Clara. It hurts. Where's the pink bottle? Fuck the pink bottle—I want some brandy. (What do you think of that, Doctor Kildare?) Stomach. Shut up. Angry? Me? No. What makes you say that? Not angry. Well then what? German dog scares baby. So? Baby bites dog. (That was easy.) "I bless America . . ." "Go to school, Clara, be a good girl—be like everybody else. Speekity lickity fast de English. Have a hot dog, Clara. This is your life now, here—America. The other was just a dream." Oh yeah? My brother's the King of Moscow, you know.

We hear the voices of a young woman and a male dog walker.

VOICE OF YOUNG WOMAN Excuse me but that's against the law.

VOICE OF MALE DOG WALKER Why don't you mind your own business?

VOICE OF YOUNG WOMAN You're supposed to clean up after it.

CLARA (*chiming in, shouting*) And besides it's disgusting! Some of us live out here, you know. Eat it! Stomach. Not again. Yes. Back. Back too? Yes. Shit. Yeah, maybe that too. The deli? They won't let you. Shit on their floor, then, who cares. "Sing that song from where you come from," they scream. "Sing 'Melancholy Baby.'" I won't. But I sing to the gravel in the driveway. "Sing to me, my melancholy baby . . ." Then I go upstairs, take a bath, make myself tired and go lie on my bed. Myra asks, "Don't you have any homework to do?" "Homework hurts," I tell her. It's what goes through my head so I say it: "Homework hurts Clara." Myra looks at Al. Al looks at Myra. I'm fifteen. They think I'm retarded. Retarded? Why not? I say a few more things like that and they leave me alone.

We hear the voice of a young person passing by.

VOICE OF YOUNG PERSON He actually dropped acid and amphetamine *together*. Can you *imagine* what that was like?

CLARA No. Can't stand the suburbs. What's a junior high school anyway? A loony bin for kids, right? Myra volunteers to play the part of my mother in English in Chicago. She takes me to the doctor. I've heard about needles. The camps. I shove his instrument tray over, punch his nurse in the ear. "Nobody can blame you for not having this child in your home, Mrs. Bernstein." Fuck you, Doctor Kildare. Fuck you, Myra. Next thing Japetto *pays* to play the part of my father. New Brunswick, New Jersey. Can't stand the suburbs. Japetto tries to touch me. So I bite him. Fuck you, Japetto. Baby bites dog. Should have bitten it off. "She's violent," he screams. So they tie me up and lock me in a hospital. Needles for breakfast. Needles for lunch. Needles at night. I won't take pills. They can't force me. I won't let a man put his fingers in my mouth, or a woman either. Nobody does that to me. (*She speaks to someone passing by.*) What am I doing? What does it look like I'm doing? I'm flying over the George Washington Bridge inspecting the Hudson River. (*She speaks to us again.*) When I get out they get me a job as a waitress. "Pretend you're real, Clara. Faster. Smile. Don't smile. Don't spill." *Me,* playing a waitress? Fuck you, Japetto. My part of playing a waitress lasts two days. I catch a bus to New York. This place I can go incognito. (*She addresses a person passing by.*) Just waiting. For what? For nothing. Just waiting. Just talking. No offense. Just here for a while. No offense.

The person passing is gone.

Fuck you, Japetto. They don't kill you outright in those places, 'cause someone might find out. They kill you with drugs and needles, torture you like in the camps. "Clara, if you start a thought, you must finish it. Don't interrupt yourself, Clara. It doesn't make sense." But if I'm in the loony bin, I must be loony—so why make sense? When I think something I don't like: wipe, good-bye, so long, it's gone. What was I saying? I forget. Wipe. That's all. Good-bye.

From the street we hear the voices of a child and an adult.

VOICE OF A CHILD   Is she one of the purple people?

VOICE OF AN ADULT   No, she's a bag lady.

VOICE OF A CHILD   Where are the purple people?

VOICE OF AN ADULT   Collecting dung from the policemen's horses.

VOICE OF A CHILD   Why?

VOICE OF AN ADULT   They grow mushrooms in it.

A rumbling subway sound is becoming evident.

CLARA   Some of us know everything but we don't tell. If you tell, they kill you. They come when I talk too much. They march inside my head. They trample all over my brain with their big boots. I try to faint but I can't always. That's when I go to the shelter for a night. But that's humiliating, you know? They make you leave your things outside. You can't drink. You can't smoke. Who do they think they are? And what if they find out I know everything? They'd harness me to a computer. "Be a good girl, Clara. Be like everybody else. *This* is your life now, Clara, here." "I bless America . . ." Stomach. Never mind.

Clara is struggling not to acknowledge unpleasant messages from her body. There are eruptive sounds from the street.

Salvation Army, move on, move on. You're blocking the view. Boat. Train. Why couldn't she come? Papers . . . papers. Wipe. Statue of Liberty. Stumbles. Gasps. Retrieves. Wipe. Elizabeth Taylor, Catherine the Great—I play them all. Over and out. Roger. Roger, order me another baked potato, please, I'm going to the john. Bless you. *Pas de quoi*, my dear. Itching again. Scratch. Better. Feels better. "Answer my question." What question? "I'm asking you a question, Clara." Well, what? Sugar with my coffee, honey, yes. Pile of shit. Hey! What is this, a tip? Pile of shit. Thank you. What for? Don't touch me. Stomach. Puke. Shit. All systems red. Alert the navigator!!!

Siren sounds.

What's that? The A. The A again on its way to the Battery. On its way to America full of children, full of children, stopping at Forty-second Street, stopping at the camp. They don't kill you outright 'cause someone might find out. Tear down the hospitals! There's one medicine they give you to shut you up which if you have the runs and you keep taking this medicine you shit yourself to death and they don't tell you. "Your mama will come see you, Clara, when the train stops at the camp. She'll come say good-bye, Clara." We'll save this piece of bread for Mama. Mama is at the camp waiting. The A train will stop at the camp. All the children will say good-bye to their mamas and papas. "Here's the camp, Clara, aren't you excited?" *Cher Monsieur* Morganstern— (*She is searching with increasing desperation for something precious in one of her bags.*) Where is Mama? Where is Mama? I don't see her. "The papers didn't come through in time, Clara. Not her fault. She couldn't—" Mama!

The street is fairly quiet. Clara is panicked looking for her object.

The one out there. He's the one! His hand in his pocket. Call the police. He *is* the police. Black boot. This is it. This is where they get her. The one in the overcoat. He's the one. Black boot. Get out of here. Look the other way. Don't look in his eyes. He won't see you. The A train: I want it to go faster and faster with all the children in it. When it crashes, all the children will be dead: no sound, disappeared, no trace. Just me, Clara, sitting right here. Black boot. They're talking about her. Black boots. They're coming. No, they're waiting for later, planning, talking about me. Don't look at them. Be a crazy. Be a good quiet crazy. Smile, shut up. Clara, if you want to sleep, put your bags around you, you'll be safe. But the dream . . . Something dark and slimy is oozing itself over her. Something dark and slimy is curving over her, a soft darkness is reaching his hand around her to cover her mouth! Scream, Clara, scream! Can't. Try. Can't. Try. Scream backwards, inwards. Gasp. Bite! Bite into the darkness! (*Clara finds what she's looking for. She carefully unwraps layers of tissue paper from around a small black bag. From the bag she takes out an old doll's head, its body mostly gone. Clara talks to the doll.*) What is it, Clara? What is it, dear? Everything's all right. Where is Clara? She's right here, Mama. Clara has Mama's arms. Mama's legs are all packed away with the other legs. Clara knows where they are. Don't worry, Mama. Clara knows where they are. Don't blame Clara. Clara hasn't lost them. She didn't tear them off. Nobody's going to take Mama away. We'll wrap her up now. Nobody will touch Mama. Clara's a good girl. No train will come. Clara's a good girl. She'll take care of Mama. She won't hurt her. (*As she wraps up the doll again, she sings to it softly, a few lines of a Russian lullaby.*) "Come on in, Clara, the water's fine." No thanks, Mama, I'll just sit here. What was that? Nothing, Clara. It's quiet. Too quiet. I'm on the yacht, listening to the waves. No sleeping tonight. Keep watch. It's wartime. (*Clara tells us a story.*) At four in the morning once I saw a long white truck, the longest white truck I ever saw, come rolling through here on cotton wheels, so quiet, with police cars. "Wide load" in front, in back. Full of Nazi brains. When that truck shakes a little, Nazi brains go out into the air. And we're breathing it. We've all got some Nazi brains in us now. How can we get it off the planet? Send it off in a rocket ship? But if that rocket explodes, then all that Nazi mind all over everything. Can't bury it. Earth doesn't want it—don't want to be eating Nazi vegetables. Can't put it in the ocean—don't want to drink Nazi water. What to do with Nazi brains? You can't get rid of them. And we're breathing it. We've all got some Nazi brains in us now. (*She speaks to someone on the street.*) I hiss, you know. Don't you know it's not good manners to stare at crazies? (*She talks to us again.*) Want to know what's going to happen? I'll tell you. Everybody should know. Things'll look the same for a few years. Then suddenly they'll look different. (*She is starting to pack up*.) Sick people'll be giving out prescriptions. No more doctors; all dead from their own drugs. Trucks'll be stalled on the sidewalks. People sleeping in shifts. Nobody'll have names anymore. Suddenly somebody—me maybe—will stand on top of a truck and shout: "That's all, folks. Go home. City's over. Everybody leaves." No more Fourteenth Street. No more buses. No more movies. No more drugstores. No more Forty-second Street. No more nothing. Blackout. Standstill. Walk out on the tops of cars. My boots. Put them on. Take only what you can carry. Walk to the bus station, use the ladies' room. My little bag. Good. Only essentials.

Lights fade out as Clara finishes packing.

THE TIBETAN BOOK
OF THE DEAD,
OR HOW NOT TO
DO IT AGAIN

adapted from translations of Tibetan texts

photo by Gerry Vezzuso

The Tibetan Book of the Dead, or How Not to Do It Again premiered at LaMama Experimental Theater Club in New York City, January 14, 1983, directed by Assurbanipal Babilla and produced by Ellen Stewart. Set, Jun Maeda; music, Steve Gorn; acting consultant, Priscilla Smith; literary assistant, Edith Goldenhar; floor mandala painting, Louise Baum. Performers: Cristobal Carambo, Du-Yee Chang, Sussan Deihim, Kevin O'Meara, Hooshang Touzie, Ching Valdez and Robinson Youngblood.

In 1996 the script of the play became the libretto for an opera, with music composed by Ricky Ian Gordon: *The Tibetan Book of the Dead, or The Great Liberation Through Hearing.* The play is published as an illustrated book with production photos by Gerry Vezzuso: *The Tibetan Book of the Dead for Reading Aloud,* North Atlantic Press, 1998. The acting version of *The Tibetan Book of the Dead* is available from Dramatists Play Service, 440 Park Avenue South, NY, NY 10016, which controls stock and amateur performance rights. Copyright *The Tibetan Book of the Dead* 1983 by Jean-Claude van Itallie.

INTRODUCTION

The Tibetan Book of the Dead is a manual traditionally read aloud to the dying and the dead by a spiritual teacher or a friend. It is a teaching expressed through the spoken word.

One of the earliest teachers to bring Buddhism to Tibet, Padmasambhava, popularly called Precious Guru (*Guru Rinpoche*), is said to have composed *The Tibetan Book of the Dead* around the eighth century A.D. It was rediscovered in Tibet as a Hidden Treasure (*Terton*) around six hundred years ago and is part of the everyday culture of Tibetan Buddhism.

The Tibetan Book of the Dead contains practical navigational instructions of urgent use on the journey that starts with dying and continues in the days following death. A guidebook to the "in-between place," it instructs how to avoid the suffering caused by the confusion of constantly discursive thoughts.

The Tibetan Book of the Dead is also for the living, a meditation manual on how to pay attention despite the distractions of our daily worlds.

In *The Tibetan Book of the Dead,* the traveler-after-death starts "at the top" with an experience of the clear white light of universal mind. This light, most visible at the moment of death, is our best opportunity. If we recognize it as our own fully awakened nature, we may merge with it.

If we do not, however, the five peaceful manifestations of universal energy each appear in turn. (Presumably these energies appear differently to each person.) Pay attention, says *The Tibetan Book of the Dead*—these peaceful energies are you too.

But if we don't recognize these as emanations of our own mind, then the five universal energies will appear again, this time in angry form.

If, despite warnings from the *Book,* we are blinded by fear and do not recognize the angry energies as emanations of our own mind, we descend further yet. We attempt to return to our former body. We want our possessions back. The voice of a friend reading the *Book* aloud reminds us that we can't return to the past, that we must be fearless, that we must take this opportunity not to be reborn into a world of tears.

But if we allow ourselves to be pushed even further downward by demons, by old habits of thinking, then we must seek refuge in a womb. "Don't grab just any womb," says the *Book*. The *Book* gives the dead one instructions on how to consciously choose an auspicious place of rebirth.

The Tibetan Book of the Dead reminds us, in living as in dying, to stay alert, to be fearless and undistracted.

The Tibetan Book of the Dead addresses us as "Nobly Born" and "You of Glorious Origin," reminding us that we are ourselves manifestations of universal energy.

Jean-Claude van Itallie

for my teachers
Chogyam Trungpa, Rinpoche
and
Ellen Stewart
with love and respect

As the audience enters they can see the actors and the musicians preparing.
The back of the stage is a ceiling-high skull. In front of the skull the floor is
painted with a four-part mandala or circle. A small handmade table and
chair sit on a rug toward the front. An offering table with a flower and a
little rice in a bowl is near the musicians' platform. An actor is outlining the
perimeter of the floor mandala with chalk. The musicians tune and try out
instruments.

THE DYING

The lights dim slowly. Two actors slowly walk a long faded violet winding
sheet around the perimeter of the painted floor mandala. They place the
winding sheet on the actor who will play the dying one. The dying one
faces the audience. During the dying the musicians provide a subtle sound
reminiscent of breathing. An actor standing in the center of the mandala
addresses the audience as if they were friends of the dying one.

Oh you,
Who have come to this place,
Sisters and brothers, friends,
This person is dying.
She (he) has not chosen to do so.
She is suffering greatly.
She has no home, no friends.
Falling as from a cliff,
She is entering a strange forest.

The actors, standing on various parts of the mandala, show concern for the dying one as she walks very slowly toward the front. They murmur prayers in various languages.

Driven by the winds, swept by the ocean,
She feels no solid ground.
She is embarking on a great battle.
Moved from state to state,
She is alone and helpless.
Embrace her with your love.

Another actor accompanies and addresses the dying one.

My friend,
You are feeling heavy.
You can no longer open or close your eyes.
Blue, yellow, red and green are turning white.
Logic and the chair and the table are dissolving.

An actor addresses the dying one.

The earth element in your body is dissolving into water.

The actor accompanying the dying one addresses her.

My friend,
Your mind is losing its hold.
You grab at this,
You grab at that.
Your blood is slowing,
You feel faint.
Logic and the chair and the table are dissolving.

An actor takes away the small chair. Another actor takes away the small table.

No more external sounds,
No more internal sounds.
You have no saliva, no sweat.
Everything is drying.

An actor addresses the dying one.

The water element in your body is dissolving into fire.

The actor accompanying the dying one addresses her.

My friend,
Now you feel cold.
You have a sense of far-off vastness,
And you seem to see fireflies, or sparks
Within smoke.
You can't get enough air.
You are losing ground.
Everything seems hollow.

As the dying one is about to kneel on a small rug, an actor pulls it away.

You try to remember who you love.

The actors start to make a low humming sound. An actor addresses the dying one.

The fire element in your body is dissolving into air.

The actor accompanying the dying one addresses her.

My friend,
Now you are losing your last touch with the world:
Your sense of taste.

An actor runs in with a candle in a brass holder. The candle is held near the dying one.

The last sign:
A sputtering butter lamp,
About to go out.

The actor holding the candle blows it out. Another actor addresses the dying one.

The air element in your body is dissolving into ether.

The candle is taken away. The dying one remains standing.

THE MOMENT OF DEATH

A white scarf is laid over the dying one's head, covering her face but open at the sides. An actor holds a book and reads from it into the dying one's ear. The music builds.

My friend,
Now is the moment of death.

The time has come for you to start out.
You are going home.

Oh, Nobly Born,
Now is the moment.
Before you is mind, open and wide as space,
Simple, without center or circumference.

Now is the moment of death.
Your mind in this moment is total transparency:
No color, no substance, empty,
Sparkling, pure and vibrant,
A mass of light
Not stopped by any obstacle.
It has neither beginning nor end.
Go toward the light.
Merge with it.
Merge with the light.

Death has happened.
It happens to everyone.

CLEAR WHITE LIGHT

From high up at the back of the stage, from the third eye of the huge skull, a single bright light shines at the audience for about twelve seconds. The light goes out. Immediately an actor speaks urgently to the audience, as if the audience were the dead one.

Merge with the clear white light.
Don't long for what's finished.
You can't stay here anymore.
Death has happened.
It happens to everyone.
In this crucial moment,
Don't be afraid.
Whatever appears,
Recognize as the form of your own thoughts.

With urgency another actor runs to speak to the audience.

Please don't be afraid of your own radiance.
You no longer have a physical body.
Death has happened.
So nothing can hurt you.
You can't die again.
Don't be afraid.
Merge with the light. Merge. Merge.

THE PEACEFUL ENERGIES

The music marks a change. An actor addresses the audience.

As you have not merged with the clear white light,
The five families, the universal energies,
Will now appear
In peaceful aspect, each in turn.

The dead one—who may be played by a different actor now—the white scarf hanging vertically over his face, stands in the center of the mandala on the white circle. Around him five actors move subtly, like electrons circling a nucleus. One actor squats near the musicians' platform, holding the book. He or she reads to the dead one. From now until the end of the play whichever actor plays the dead one will wear the white scarf.

In the center
You find a place to make camp,
A place where others have been before you,
A muddy field between winter and spring.

The reader chants.

Now the clear white sky of All-Embracing Wisdom
Spreads everywhere without a center.

The reader reads.

The great emperor with his consort
Arises in the center of your being.

In the center the five actors slowly form the shape of the Vairocana, who, like all the energies the dead one will encounter, is created by actors' bodies. Each of the five peaceful energies will appear as a different grouping of king, queen and court. Vairocana and his consort are monumental and stonelike, emperor and empress. Slow percussive sounds. The light is white. Vairocana traditionally holds a wheel, so the actors move like a great wheel. Vairocana traditionally has four faces, one to each direction. Musical punctuation as an actor goes to each direction and speaks its name, starting with East and ending with South, which faces the audience.

East.
North.
West.
South.

The reader chants to the dead one.

Now the clear white sky of All-Embracing Wisdom spreads.
The great emperor with his consort
Arises in the center of your being.

The dead one steps outside the center circle and watches, stunned by the radiance of Vairocana. The reader reads to the dead one.

Oh, Noble One, do not separate yourself from him.

An actor breaks out of the Vairocana grouping, playing the role of the tempter, holding up one hand as if it were a little boat, enticing the dead one with it, drawing him in a circle around Vairocana. Elsewhere on stage a single white lightbulb blinks; we hear a bit of bliss realm music, which we will hear again later. The reader reads to the dead one.

Oh, Noble One, do not be frightened.
Abandon all fixed points of view.
Be like an ocean with no boat.
Be like an ocean with no boat,
All directions at once.

But if you hide in a world of bliss
You won't be able to think.
Don't pull back.
Be like an ocean with no boat,
Oh, Nobly Born.

So remain awake, oh Nobly Born.
Merge with All-Encompassing Wisdom
At the center of your being.
Merge. Merge. Merge.

For an instant the dead one turns back toward Vairocana. Then the light on the center white circle goes out, as does the blinking white bulb. In the east, the blue quadrant of the floor mandala, the actors form Akshobya, his consort and his court, all facing the dead one. The light is blue. Akshobya is the brilliant winter king. Traditionally he holds a sword and a mirror, symbols of piercing and reflecting intelligence. The actors use their hands and bodies rather than props to embody these qualities. The reader reads to the dead one.

Now in the east
The blue water element sparkles:
The Diamond One and his consort
Shine from the Realm of Complete Joy,
Unshakeable Mirrorlike Wisdom,
Lake with no ripples
Reflecting the world as it is,
Intelligence piercing your heart like an icicle.
Don't be angry, Oh Noble One.
Water will purify.
This is the sharp sword of vision,
Lightning insight,
Blue-white of winter,
Clarity of sunrise,
Diamond Mind.

From within the Akshobya group an actor breaks out and plays the tempter. He behaves as if daring the dead one to hit him, drawing the dead one in a circle around Akshobya. Elsewhere on stage a gray or smoky lightbulb is blinking and pointed to by the tempter. We hear a bit of hate realm music, with the rhythm of hard rock, which we will hear again later.

But if you are angry,
If you flee
To the smoky worlds of hate,
You'll feel such pain
You won't be able to think.

So remain alert, Oh Nobly Born.
The diamond rays are your own diamond rays.
Recognize them.
Merge. Merge. Merge.

The dead one turns back for an instant to the blue radiance of Akshobya and his court. Then the bright blue light goes out, and the blinking gray

*bulb goes out. There arises a bright golden light in the southern yellow
quadrant of the mandala, which is toward the front and where the five actors
form Ratnasambhava, his consort and his court. The dead one faces
Ratnasambhava, who is the rich sun-king of the golden harvest, generous
and regal. Traditionally Ratnasambhava holds a jewel. The reader reads to
the dead one.*

> Now from the south
> The earth element shines yellow like gold.
> From the Realm of the Great and the Glorious
> Comes the Splendid King and his court
> All bejeweled:
> The abundance of harvest,
> Generosity and wealth,
> Kingly Wisdom of Equanimity,
> The sun.
> Merge. Merge. Merge.

*From within the sun-king group, an actor playing the tempter breaks away
and draws the dead one in a circle around Ratnasambhava, tempting him as
if with a desirable object held in the tempter's hand. Elsewhere on stage a
blue lightbulb blinks, and we hear a bit of human realm music, a simple
melody which we will hear again later. The reader reads to the dead one.*

> But if you are proud
> And hide in the human world,
> You experience once again
> Birth, suffering, old age and death.
> So, Nobly Born,
> Rest in the golden rays.
> Merge. Merge. Merge.

*The dead one turns back for an instant toward the splendor of
Ratnasambhava. Then the bright golden light goes out and the light from
the blinking blue bulb goes out. In the western red, stage right quadrant of
the floor mandala a bright red light shines on the dead one and five actors
who become the fiery Amitabha with consort and court. This is the rosy red
kingdom of compassion. The reader reads to the dead one.*

Now from the west
The fire element glows everywhere red:
The sunset.
From the Realm of Ecstasy
Glows the Compassionate One on his peacock throne.
Oh, Nobly Born,
This is the warmth of your own heart.
Embrace it.
Merge. Merge. Merge.
This is springtime, blossoms,
Fawns dancing in a field,
Beauty touching your heart,
Discriminating Wisdom.
Merge. Merge.

From within the red Amitabha grouping an actor playing the tempter breaks away. She or he is seductive, attracting the dead one away from the red kingdom of compassion. Elsewhere on stage a yellow bulb blinks, and we hear a bit of "hungry ghost" realm music, a sad single jazz horn sound, which we will hear again later. The reader reads to the dead one.

But if you inflame love into desire,
You will become a hungry ghost,
Always hungry, always thirsty.
So, Nobly Born,
Rest, rest
In the rosy light of Compassion.
Merge.

The dead one turns for an instant back toward the red Amitabha group. Then the strong red light and the blinking yellow bulb go out. Upstage in the northern green quadrant of the floor mandala, the five actors form the great wind king, Amogasiddhi, his consort and his court. The five actors, bathed in green light, are like a great bird flying with many wings. The reader reads to the dead one.

Now from the green north
Arises the air element, the wind,
Stirring your heart.

From the Realm of the Accomplishment of All Actions
Comes the Great Doer,
On the back of his powerful bird,
The wings of the bird raising the wind,
Stirring the leaves,
Swaying the birches,
Rippling the green grasses of summer,
Filling your ears with sound.
Be one with this activity.
Merge. Merge.

*From within the green realm a tempter breaks away and creates envy for the
high kicks he or she performs. The dead one tries to imitate the tempter's
high kicks and is led in a circle away from the green realm of the great bird.
Elsewhere on stage a red lightbulb blinks and we hear a bit of the fast
rhythms of the competitive realm of the jealous gods, which we will hear
again later. The reader reads to the dead one.*

But if out of envy
You hide in the world of the jealous,
You'll never stop striving, reaching, competing,
Striving, reaching, competing.
So join the shining wind itself.
This the way of your own mind.

Be the wind.
Be the wind.

*For an instant the dead one turns back toward the great green bird king.
Then the bright green light and the blinking red bulb go out.*

THE RAINBOW DANCE

A reader reads to the dead one.

The peaceful energies
Appear together now, dancing.
Merge with the rainbow.

*The strong white, blue, yellow, red and green lights appear together,
forming pools of color on the floor mandala. We hear the energetic rainbow
dance music made by sour horns, cymbals and drums. The dead one stands
in the center. An actor with a white silk cloth dances the principal dance in
the front light. The five other actors each wave a silk banner of a different
color on a pole. The six different-colored lightbulbs blink. At the end of the
dance, the dead one is moving about the stage like an animal, and only the
green lightbulb, indicating the animal realm, is left blinking. The colored
lights are out. The actors remove the silk cloths from their poles and wrap
the cloths around themselves. One actor covers the dead one in a blue cloth,
then reads to the dead one.*

THE DREAMLIKE REALMS

Oh, you of glorious origin,
You saw the families of organic energy.
If you had recognized their radiance
As your own,
You would have dissolved into the rainbow.

But you are still wandering.
Don't be afraid.
The four directions of your own heart
Are old friends,
The play of your own mind.
Piercing doubt,
Free of all thoughts,
Greet them as a mother embraces her child.
They will dissolve into you
And you will attain illumination.

But if you are afraid,
And attracted again to familiar dreamlike realms,
The realms of the gods,

The jealous gods,
The humans,
The animals,
The hungry ghosts,
Or the hell beings,
Then you will be reborn
Into the ocean of miseries.

So remain free of all thoughts.

If you are drawn to the god realm,
To the dreamy world of the blissful,

The white bulb blinks. The actor wearing the white cloth moves as if in a blissful trance to the floor under the blinking white bulb. We hear the music of the blissful realm, indicating a mildly pleasant drugged-out state.

You will no longer be able to think.
So remain alert,
Oh, Nobly Born,
And watch, watch.

The white bulb goes out.

If you are pulled to the jealous god realm,
To the cloudy world of the ambitious,

The red bulb blinks. The actor wearing the red cloth rushes to it, jumping up, trying to reach it. These actions are accompanied by competitive fast music indicating the realm of the jealous gods.

Oh, Nobly Born,
You will never stop striving, reaching, competing,
Striving, reaching, competing.
So watch, watch.

The red bulb goes out.

Oh, Nobly Born,
Even if you hide in the human realm,
In the dreamy human world,

The blue bulb blinks. The dead one gets up, adjusting the blue scarf and his or her clothes, attracted by the relatively simple melody of the human realm.

Constantly adjusting this and that,
Trying to be comfortable,
You will experience once again
Birth, suffering, old age and death.
So watch, watch.

The blue bulb goes out.

And don't be attracted to the colorless animal realm,

The green bulb blinks. The actor with the green cloth circles under it like an animal, making animal sounds.

Oh, Nobly Born,
For there are no words there, no humor.
So watch, watch.

The green bulb goes out.

Oh, Nobly Born,
If you are addicted to the half-world
Of the hungry ghosts,

The yellow bulb blinks. The actor with the yellow cloth circles under it in a state of wanting, compulsively desirous—of drink, drugs, sex or whatever. We hear the haunting music of the hungry ghosts, music that might be heard in a late-night bar.

You will only desire and desire.
Never satisfied,
You will develop a large belly and a small throat.
So watch, watch.

The yellow bulb goes out.

And don't be drawn
To the smoky realms of hate,

The smoky gray bulb blinks. The actor with the gray cloth curses under his breath as he moves with increasingly angry gestures toward the gray bulb, goes under it and continues off.

Or you'll feel such pain
You won't be able to think.
So remain alert, Oh Nobly Born.
Watch, watch.

All the bulbs blink.

Don't be reborn
Into the ocean of miseries.
Remain free of all thoughts.

The reader, holding the large open book under her chin close to her face, circles until, still holding the book in the same manner, she faces the audience. The other actors stand in a group behind her, also facing the audience, cupping their hands to their mouths as if shouting. They make no sound but mouth urgently to the audience the same words the reader reads.

Oh, You of Glorious Origin,
Watch, watch.
Don't be distracted.
Don't escape the rainbow dance of your own mind.
Iti samaya rigya rigya rigya.

THE ANGRY ENERGIES

Because the dead one missed the opportunity to merge with them in their peaceful forms, the five universal energies will now appear in their angry forms. These apparitions too are an opportunity to merge with them. Five actors, lit dimly by white light in the center white circle, form the four-faced imperial Vairocana, his consort and his court. The music is a thunderlike variation of the majestic percussive music heard previously for Vairocana. The dead one, holding a candle, faces Vairocana, whose angry aspect is ignorance. The actor playing Vairocana's consort shouts to the dead one.

The five families of universal energies
Will now appear to you
In wrathful aspect,
Each thundering in turn.
Don't be terrified.

Light goes out on Vairocana. The actor who had played the consort shouts to the dead one.

The huge stonelike white demon
Mired in the center of your mind
Is your own ignorance.
Recognize it, Oh Nobly Born.

In the blue quadrant of the floor mandala, under dim blue light, the five actors form the angry hating aspect of the ice king Akshobya, his consort and his court. We hear an angry variation of the Akshobya music we heard earlier. The Akshobya group writhes in hatred. The dead one, holding the candle, tries to peer more closely at the face of the consort of Vairocana. She suddenly reaches out to pull the dead one in. The dead one pulls back in fear. The dim blue light goes out on Akshobya. The actor who had played Akshobya's consort hisses at the dead one.

The furious ice blue demon
Freezing the east of your mind
Is your own hatred.
Recognize it, Oh Nobly Born.

The dead one, holding the candle, runs in fear to another area of the theater. In the yellow quadrant under dim yellow light, the five actors form the prideful aspect of King Ratnasambhava, his queen and his court. We hear a proud variation of the kingly Ratnasambhava music we heard previously, accompanied by the five actors murmuring. The dead one, holding the candle, tries to peer into the queen's face. The yellow light on Ratnasambhava grouping goes out. The actor who had played the queen announces proudly to the dead one:

The stubborn yellow tyrant
Enthroned in the south of your mind

Is your own pride.
Recognize it, Oh Nobly Born.

The dead one, holding the candle, runs in terror behind the huge skull at the back of the stage, then reemerges fearfully from its mouth. In the red quadrant, under dim red light, the five actors form the passionate fiery aspect of Amitabha, his consort and his court. They writhe sensuously. We hear a passionate variation of the compassionate Amitabha music we heard previously. The dead one is attracted to the lustful consort of Amitabha, who tries to lure him in. The red light goes out. The actor who played the consort calls out to the dead one.

The voracious red mouth
Devouring the west of your mind
Is your own lust.
Recognize it, Oh Nobly Born.

The dead one, holding the candle, approaches fascinated and terrified as the five actors, under dim green light in the green quadrant, form the envious twisting monster Amogasiddhi, his consort and his court. We hear the active Amogasiddhi music we heard before, but with variations expressing jealousy. The actor playing the consort of Amogasiddhi shouts to the dead one.

The hideous green monster
Twisting the north of your mind
Is your own envy.
Recognize it, Oh Nobly Born.

The dim green light on the monster goes out.

MAHAKALA

The five actors have fallen in a heap on the ground. The dead one, who fled behind the skull, reappears through its mouth, moving slowly backward toward us. The dead one faces the skull's mouth, through which, like a tongue, emerges a furled red silk banner on a pole. The pole is held by an actor wearing black, playing Mahakala. A reader reads aloud.

Many-armed Mahakala,
Fierce and dark protector of wisdom,
Now appears,
Terrifying and powerful.
Recognize your darker self.

Mahakala, fierce, masculine and strong, like a shaman, emerges slowly from the skull's mouth, making deep loud sounds. Mahakala is terrifying in aspect, but in his essence he is peace. He moves slowly forward in stylized fashion, but with great energy. With magnificent strength and grace he makes great circles with his unfurled big red silk banner over the heap of actors on the floor, as if his banner could cut the thread of life of demons. As Mahakala reaches the front of the stage, the lights go out.

THE LORD OF DEATH

A reader reads aloud.

Now the Lord of Death appears.

The dead one watches from the side, holding a candle. The five actors on the ground sing softly a cappella.

"This old man, he plays one.
He plays knick-knack on my thumb,
With a knick-knack, paddy whack,
Give the dog a bone.
This old man goes rolling home."

As they sing, they slowly rise from their heap on the floor. Once they are standing they smile a bit and wave slightly toward the audience. Then they take a little step forward and fall into a silent heap. Then they rise again, slowly as before, singing the same children's verse softly. Again the actors take a step forward, smile and wave slightly, then fall into a silent heap. They are portraying the Lord of Death, who is said to hold the whole cycle of life within his jaws. Each cycle of rising and falling is like growing from child to maturity, and falling back to earth. When they have completed a third cycle, one of the actors leaves the group and walks directly up to the dead one, addressing him or her conversationally.

Oh, You of Glorious Origin, don't be afraid.
Even if you were cut into little pieces,
You couldn't possibly die again.
Emptiness cannot harm emptiness.

THE WANDERER'S PRAYER

The dead one stands listening. From behind the softly lit skull an actor sings a plaintive song, not in English. Then the dead one prays.

As I wander through worlds of illusion,
May I remain confident
And remember my own mind.

As the dead one continues, an actor hangs upside down in the mouth of the skull. In one of the skull's eye sockets an actor sits combing her hair. Two actors walk past the mouth of the skull laughing, like children playing. The mellow mood is of not much happening, of the remembered shadows and sounds of a few people doing ordinary things.

May the Five Wisdoms shine.
May I recognize myself.
When earth, water, fire, air or ether rise up against me,
May I remember my teachers.
May blessings go before me,
And compassionate Queens of Space
Help me to cross this dangerous place.
When my old ways of thinking
Cause me to wander,
May I hear blessings
Even in the roar of a thousand thunders
And recognize this realm of shadows

For what it is.
Confident, may I see the Universal Energies.
Sarva Mangalam.

REALIZING I AM DEAD

The word Sarvamangalam—*which in Sanskrit means, more or less, "So
be it," or "May there be blessings"—is taken up as a soft melodic chant by
the actors in the eye sockets of the skull. The floor mandala is lit brightly.
The dead one runs the perimeter of it, does a handstand in the center,
jumps like a child playing hopscotch from quadrant to quadrant, delighted,
as if the mandala were the whole world and he or she could jump to any
part of it. The dead one speaks to the audience.*

I saw peaceful and angry energies
But I didn't recognize them as my own,
So I fainted.
When I was alive,
I was blind, I limped, and I was mute.
But now my eyes distinguish.
My ears hear.
I can move easily.
My voice is clear.
So I know I must be dead.
If I can remember that,
I won't be lost.
I won't need to be reborn.
I no longer have a physical body.
I am wandering.
I have amazing powers.
I can go where I wish in the time it takes to open
Or close my hand.
I see my house and my friends
As if in a dream.

The dead one sees family and friends mourning in the eye sockets of the skull. The dead one calls to them.

Hello. I'm here.

They don't hear him. He tries to leap up to them.

What am I to do?
I'm like a fish on hot sand.

Hanging on a bar over the mouth of the skull, the dead one kicks his or her feet in the air, then jumps down. The Sarvamangalam *music is silent a moment; the dead one speaks.*

My mind wanders like a lost feather.

The dead one calls to family and friends again.

I'm here. Don't cry. I'm here.

They don't hear. The dead one speaks quietly.

So.
I am dead.

PURSUED BY DEMONS

There is a long high-pitched sound with percussive and wind elements. The dead one lies like a corpse across the mouth of the skull. The actors rush like demons down ladders from the eye sockets. They surround the dead one, as if eating her or his corpse. One of the actors walks to the front of the mandala carrying a large crumpled white cloth. She drops the cloth to the floor. She kneels to examine it, like a soothsayer looking into a crystal ball or reading tea leaves.

Oh, Nobly Born, the demons that pursue you now:
The mountains crumbling,
The earthquakes,
The tidal waves and fires,

The approaching armies,
The hunters and the wild beasts,
All these spring from your own mind.

The wind music rises. The dead one is as if pursued down a mountain.
The soothsayer picks up the cloth and hands it to a second soothsayer, who
drops and examines it with equal care. A warrior holding three silk
banners—one red, one black and one white—stands stock still behind the
second soothsayer. The sounds abate when she speaks.

Passion,

The warrior holds forward the red banner.

Aggression

The warrior holds forward the black banner.

And Ignorance:

The warrior holds forward the white banner.

Three cliffs.
You are about to fall.
Oh, Nobly Born, recognize the state of becoming.

The light goes out on the warrior. The dead one—again a different actor
playing the dead one—stands near the center of the mandala. Other actors
form a funeral procession, walking slowly around the edge of the mandala,
carrying a wooden pallet with a white cloth draped over what might be a
body. The funeral march is solemn, percussive. The dead one speaks.

I see my home and my friends,
But they cannot see me.
So I must be dead.
Where is my body?

An actor echoes.

Where is my body?

The dead one speaks.

Winter has frozen my corpse,
Or summer decomposed it.
Where is my body?

An actor echoes.

Where is my body?

The dead one speaks.

My friends have burned it,
Or fed it to the birds.

The dead one calls to a mourner.

Where is my body?

The mourner stops for a moment, thinking she might have heard a faint sound. Another actor echoes.

Where is my body?

The frightened mourner hurries to catch up with the funeral procession. The dead one speaks.

I feel squeezed between rocks
And tossed by the winds.
I want my body.

The actors dump the "body" they have been carrying on the wooden pallet. The "body" is a jumble of mannequin limbs and heads. The actors stand the pallet on its end and from behind it taunt the dead one. One of them moves toward the dead one like a wind-up toy. Another tries to interest the dead one in various combinations of limbs and heads, speaking incomprehensibly without moving his or her lips. The actors laugh at the dead one. Then they leave. The dead one tries to sit quietly. On either side of the dead one a judge comes to sit—one male and one female judge, like parents. The female judge opens a small black cloth in which there are white stones. The male judge opens a small white cloth in which there are black stones. An actor tiptoes in behind the dead one, holding up a small scale. In this scene the attitude toward the dead one is of friendly teasing. The female judge speaks, touching the dead one with a white stone.

One good deed.

The dead one looks at her. The male judge speaks, touching the dead one with a black stone

One bad deed.

The dead one looks at him. Each time either judge speaks, he or she touches the dead one with a stone, and the dead one looks at the judge. The female judge speaks.

One good deed.

The male judge speaks.

One bad deed.

The female judge speaks.

One good deed.

The male judge speaks.

One bad deed.

The dead one looks at him, then back toward the female judge, but she has no more white stones. The male judge speaks again.

One bad deed.

And again.

One bad deed.

The dead one keeps looking from one judge to the other, but only the male judge has stones left. The male judge keeps repeating "One bad deed" and jabbing the dead one with a stone. The female judge repeatedly pinches the dead one. The dead one's head moves back and forth, faster and faster, between the judges. Feeling tortured, the dead one cries out.

No, it's not true, not that many.

The judges leave. Behind the dead one, four actors demonically prance about the mandala. They speak matter-of-factly.

Oh, Nobly Born, you can't die now.
You have no body. You're already dead.
The demons are your own imagining.
Truly, you are empty.
Oh, Nobly Born,
Emptiness is terrifying, it's true,
But emptiness is light,
And light is only mind,
So don't be afraid.
Oh, You of Glorious Origin, watch out.
If you allow yourself to be distracted,
You will fall into a trap.

The dead one is agonized.

From moment to moment
I hurt, I want.
Back, forth, hurt, want, hurt, want.

All the demons leave except one, who, holding a mirror, speaks from behind the dead one. The demon moves lightly as she speaks, in response to music of reed instrument and drum.

The ritual for the dead is carried out for you.
Its performance is less than perfect.
Don't attach yourself to this imperfection.
Watch out. Mindless anger is a trap.
You worry: do your friends love you?
Watch out. Mindless passion is a trap.
The impurities you see in the ceremony

She kneels, holding the mirror up to the dead one's face.

Are your own face
Reflected in a mirror.

The dead one looks in the mirror. A gong sounds as the two figures are beautifully silhouetted by lights. The demon continues to speak to the dead one.

Your spirit is light now.
It moves. It has no anchor.
Every thought radiating from you has power.
Don't pity yourself.
Don't make yourself small.
You want your things
But they are of no use to you now.
Let whoever has them have them.
By wanting and wanting
You become a hungry ghost.

HUNGRY GHOSTS

The blinking yellow bulb is on. The actors, positioned in different places on the mandala and skull, pose like addicted demons in a Hieronymus Bosch painting. A single horn plays the hungry ghost music which we heard briefly earlier. A spotlight illuminates first one actor and then another, making a pass over the audience too, and catching the dead one looking for a hiding place. With the music softer, an actor approaches and speaks quietly to the dead one, whose face is half in shadow.

You come to a hiding place at last.
You think you are happy.

The white bulb blinks.

But listen. This is important:
Be careful.
You could be born here
And have to suffer life again.
So far you've not recognized your own light.

Do so now.
Close the entrance to the womb.
Even now there is no need to be reborn.
You have no body to cast a shadow.
Oh, Nobly Born,
If you are pulled to the half-world of the hungry ghosts
You will only want and want and want,
And never be satisfied.
In the lake of your own mind
There is no moon reflected.

Like a full moon, the spotlight climbs slowly up the skull to the ceiling of the theater. It stops a moment. The spotlight goes out.

LOVEMAKING

There is a different energy present, brighter light. Near the face of the skull, the actors look at each other. One bursts out laughing. A musician starts a joyous little rhythm on a wooden xylophone. An actor calls out to another. Laughter and activity: the actors set out colored cloths and cushions and a little table with food and candles. A short groom's poncho is placed over the head of a male actor. An actor is dressed in a bride's vest. The dead one watches fascinated. The wedding party does not see the dead one. The bride and groom are seated in the center. Behind them male actors hold up a long cloth. The male actors jokingly writhe and posture like women in a harem. Rice is thrown at the couple. Cheers. The music builds in earthy excitement as the bridal couple, on their knees, slowly start a rhythmic lovemaking dance. An actor who has remained near the musicians' platform sings or chants to the dead one.

Oh, You of Glorious Origin,
Don't be distracted.
Ride the horse of bliss and emptiness
Which is your own mind.
Hold the bridle tight,

227

And thus close the opening to the womb.
You see couples making love.
Don't be distracted.
Don't get caught between man and woman.
If you were conceived now
You could be born
A horse, a bird, a dog,
A horse, a bird, a dog,
A horse, a bird, a dog.
If you were born male,
You could be angry at your father,
And want your mama, your mama, your mama,
Mama, mama, mama.
If you were born female,
You could be jealous of your mother,
And want your papa, your papa, your papa,
Papa, papa, papa.

The dead one is standing near the bridal couple, moving in their rhythm.

For an instant you would know the bliss
Of sperm meeting egg.
Then you'd develop until
Your body left the womb of your mama, mama, mama.
What could be more terrifying?
What could be more terrifying?

The actors holding the cloth behind the couple drop it. Like fauns they leap around the perimeter of the mandala. The music reaches toward climax— reaches it—and stops. The amused actors catch their breath. The dead one cups his hand to his ear and leans toward the singer, as if asking what happened. The singer cups her hands to her mouth to call, but speaks quietly.

Father, mother, the great storm:
All are illusion.

WANDERING

The actors pick up the cloths, cushions and little table and put them away at the base of the skull. The dead one dances slowly to soft slow pulsing music from the back of the stage to the front. The dead one speaks in a language we cannot understand, but behind the dead one, also dancing slowly, an actor translates.

I've wandered so long
In this muddy swamp.
If I continue to see
What is transparent,
What shimmers, as solid
I will wander farther yet.
My mind itself is only an idea.
It has never been anything more.
I hear only echoes,
I see only dreams.
Cities are mirages.
The mountains are like the moon reflected in water,
Waves of my own mind.
This mind, shimmering, transparent,
Without beginning,
Without obstacle,
Is like water poured into water,
Water poured into water.

The dead one timidly takes a bow and starts to leave. A reader shouts from the back.

You are afraid.

The reader reads in a normal voice.

You hide in a big house or in a tree,
Or in the cavity of a flower.
Out of fear, to escape your demons,

You are willing to endure anything,
To take whatever body comes.
Oh, You of Glorious Origin,
Best is to rest, empty.

The dead one moves closer to the reader, who speaks more softly.

Best is to rest, empty.

The dead one moves closer yet to the reader, who whispers in the dead one's ear.

Best is to rest, empty.

The dead one reacts like a child, refusing or being unable to do what the reader suggests.

Or, if you can't, join the play of illusion.

The dead one picks up a piece of cloth, hides under it.

Don't attach yourself to this or that.
Becoming illusion's child,
The time has come to choose a body.

CHOOSING A HOME

There is the sound of a bell, then a soft drumming heartbeat starts. Four actors stand in a semicircle. The dead one examines each of their bodies. Two actors speak in unison to the dead one from down left.

Your future is beginning to outline itself.
Watch out.
Don't take whatever body appears.
Your future will be colored by
The dreamlike realm that most attracts you:
The realm
Of the gods,

The jealous gods,
The humans,
The animals,
The hungry ghosts,
Or the hell beings.
Watch out.
If you are drawn to cow dung,
Its odor will seem sweet,
And you will be born in a field of dung.
So be careful.
Choose a body to help all living beings.
Be born for the good of all.
Choose now but watch what you choose.
A good home
May be taken for a bad one.
A bad home
May be taken for a good one.

*Cold precise music of clocks and bells. On the blue eastern quadrant of the
floor mandala a blue rug is placed under blue light, and on it a small table
and chair. An actor kneels by the table and beckons to the dead one to come
inspect the rug. The actor speaks like a Near Eastern rug merchant.*

In the east: a lake with geese.

The dead one is enthusiastic.

Watch out.
That world may seem full of happiness,
But truth does not flourish there.

*Gong sound. The blue light goes out. A red light comes up on the red
western quadrant of the floor mandala. A red rug is placed there. The chair
and the table are placed on the rug. An actor sits on the table and beckons
to the dead one. The actor has the drawl of a cowboy from the American
West.*

In the west: a lake with horses.

The dead one is enthusiastic.

Watch out.
That world has many joys,
But truth does not flourish there.

Gong sound. The red light goes out. Percussive music. A green light comes up on the green northern quadrant of the floor mandala. A green rug is placed there. The chair and the table are placed on the rug. An actor stands on the rug, his arms crossed over his chest. He speaks like a New England farmer.

In the north, life is long and peaceful
By a lake with trees and cows.

The dead one is enthusiastic.

But watch out.
Truth does not flourish there.

Gong sound. The green light goes out. A golden light dawns on the yellow southern (downstage) quadrant of the floor mandala. A yellow rug is placed there. The chair and the table are placed on the rug. An actor reads to the dead one, the one about to be reborn.

In the south: a palace.

We hear the gentle melody of the human realm which we heard previously. The one about to be reborn looks to the reader, expecting to be disappointed again. But instead . . .

Enter here like a queen (king),
If you can.

The one about to be reborn walks to the table and chair. The reader is behind him or her.

Enter again this theater of illusion,
This vale of tears.

The blue and white bulbs start blinking.

Walk with your head high.
Call on the forces of compassion.

The human realm melody continues. The one about to be reborn, inspecting this southern home, squats on the small table.

ENTERING AGAIN

An actor reads to the one about to be reborn.

Enter again
The palace encrusted with gems.
Walk knowingly
In the pleasure gardens:
Bubble of illusion.
Rest in the golden rays.
Sarvamangalam.

All the other actors stand in a semicircle behind the one about to be reborn. Accompanied by music, they sing the word Sarvamangalam *again and again as a blessing song. The one about to be reborn gives each of the others a farewell embrace, then squats on the small table, looking out front. He or she jumps forward off the table. There is a loud continuing sour horn sound. The one being born, innocent and awed, drops the white scarf, walks slowly forward, each step accompanied by a deep drumbeat, then sits on the chair, still looking slightly bewildered. The other actors are welcoming, approving, affectionate. They kneel or stand near the chair, as if posing for a family portrait. The drumbeat quickens. The lights go out.*

THE TRAVELER

David Threlfall rehearsing *The Traveler*

The Traveler premiered at the Mark Taper Forum, Los Angeles, in March 1987, produced by Gordon Davidson. The cast included John Glover, Gretchen Corbett, John Cameron Mitchell and Glenn Berenbeim. In 1988 *The Traveler* was produced in England by David Laxton at the Haymarket Theatre, Leicester, and at the Almeida in London, with David Threlfall and Morag Hood, directed by Keith Boak.

CAST OF CHARACTERS

THE TRAVELER: forties

AARON: the Traveler's friend, forties

JODIE MOSES: the Traveler's sister, fifties

PAUL: the Traveler's nephew, teens

DOCTOR STEIFF: cardiologist, forties or fifties

LAURIE: recovery room nurse, twenties

MOIRA: private duty nurse, fifties

DOCTOR TINA SULLIVAN: neurologist and speech therapist, twenties

INFERNO SOULS, DOCTORS, NURSES, ORDERLY, OTHER PATIENTS

The play may be performed with a cast of eight.

As the main character in The Traveler *is a composer, the play unfolds in a world of music and of ordinary sound that in a composer's ear might become music. (The music in* The Traveler *is never saccharine-sweet, melodramatic, rock, synthesized, weird, atonal or stereotypical.)*

The choreography is spare: an image may appear to the Traveler, as if crossing the stage of his mind, and then be gone.

The Traveler's New York City apartment. Beethoven blares from the stereo on the unpainted bookshelves. The phone on the old wooden worktable is off the hook. Scattered about are many books, papers, notebooks, audio tapes, a dried flower in an old Perrier bottle, an ashtray, cigarettes, an old wooden flute, a smudged water glass with red wine in it, a smudged glass mug with coffee, partially eaten junk food and crumpled pages of the Village Voice *and the* New York Times.

The Traveler, an intense, charismatic man in his forties wearing a faded sweatshirt, is searching for something. He picks up the phone receiver and speaks.

TRAVELER   Wait a minute. (*He is searching for something. He is tense.*) Can't find it. Wait. (*In the wastebasket, he finds a crumpled newspaper page.*) I've got it—here. (*He smooths the page and reads a review, loading his voice with the sarcasm he feels is intended by the reviewer.*) ". . . but the ultimate effect on this reviewer of the highly touted Mr. Moses's admittedly subtle music, as made evident again in his *Manhattan Inferno* yesterday evening, was, despite Moses's brilliance, or perhaps because of it, soporific." *Sleep:* he's saying he went to sleep during my *Inferno*. But it's *New York Magazine.* I'm telling you I don't want him to review anything I do ever again. Hold on. (*He puts Linda on hold, speaks to another caller. His hands are always busy jotting a note, searching for something, playing with his tapes or the volume of the music or putting something into his mouth.*) Hello? (*He adopts a friendly tone.*) Yeah, Sergio, sure I remember you. I'm fine. Why? (*As he speaks, he rifles through his things to find his appointment book and a pen. In passing, he takes a bite of donut and a sip of coffee.*) Yeah, I read it. I thought it was a pretty good review—sure. (*He crumples the review again, tosses it away.*) I'm workin' on an opera now, a real opera: Yeah, *Lear.* William Shakespeare. That's right, an opera of

237

King Lear. About time, hunh? No one big since Verdi—yeah, New York—a commission. Sure, we can talk about it. Okay, four-thirty on Tuesday. (*He writes in his appointment book.*) But I'll need to be out of here at five-thirty. Can't before that—I've got a meeting. Okay, lookin' forward. So long. (*He goes back to his original call.*) Sorry, Linda. Look, can you ask Anchorage for more money? If I have to freeze my butt off for three whole days—(*His door buzzer sounds.*) I'm sorry—just a minute— (*He goes over to press the intercom "speak" button.*) Who is it?

AARON'S VOICE (*over the intercom*)   It's Aaron.

TRAVELER (*feeling pressured, to himself*)   No, no, not today. (*He presses the "enter" button.*) I'm going nuts here. (*He holds his old flute, remaining still for a long moment, breathing quietly, listening to the taped music. The doorbell rings. He turns up the volume on the music, and shouts.*) It's open.

Aaron comes in. He's about the Traveler's age, elegant in a bright scarf and forties fedora. He carries a worn leather carryall shopping bag with a potted blooming plant in it.

TRAVELER (*not turning around toward Aaron*)   Hi.

Aaron hugs the Traveler from behind.

AARON   Hi.

The Traveler pulls away a little.

AARON   Just came by to tell you—my European tour . . . (*Aaron moves the plant from his bag to the worktable.*)

TRAVELER (*perfunctorily*)   Thanks.

AARON (*excited*)   Contract signed. Finally. Three weeks. Paris, Zurich and Amsterdam. Tiny clubs, but . . .

TRAVELER (*not so interested*)   That's great. (*He gives Aaron a quick hug, then turns back to his table.*) Linda wants me to hold out for more money from Anchorage.

AARON (*looking out the window*) You want to walk out on the pier? The sun is setting.

TRAVELER I can't. (*He is suddenly inspired: he can kill two birds with one stone.*) But how about Tuesday at five-fifteen? We can go for a walk then. There'll be an interviewer here from Italy, Sergio, but forty-five minutes is my limit for anybody. So when you get here, you can tell him we're having dinner.

AARON Are we?

The Traveler fiddles with the plant.

TRAVELER Am I free for dinner on Tuesday? Is that what you're asking me? No, I'm not. (*Irritated, he moves the plant from the table to the bookshelf.*)

AARON Why don't you just check.

TRAVELER (*suppressing fury*) All right. (*He glances at his date book, is triumphant.*) Yo-Yo Ma at Avery Fisher.

AARON Who are you going with?

TRAVELER Aaron, is this an inquisition?

AARON I thought we could go together. That's all. Dinner and a concert? Is that so weird?

TRAVELER We *can* go together—on Tuesday to the record store at five-fifteen. I need some records. (*looking in his book again, impatient, with controlled anger*) And I'm free till six-thirty.

AARON (*not-so-controlled anger*) After which "blackout," right? Scene change?

TRAVELER That's right. I keep my life in separate compartments. You've told me that before. (*He picks up an extinguished half-smoked cigarette.*)

AARON I'm sorry I asked. You are a pain in the ass.

TRAVELER   Is that why you came up here? To make me feel guilty? Are you trying to write my lyrics again?

AARON   Stop it! Don't turn everything upside down. I don't want to play this scene again.

TRAVELER   Just because you have nothing to do for dinner on Tuesday, am I supposed to change my plans?

AARON   You're crazy. You're completely impossible.

TRAVELER   Are you my mother or something? Do I owe you? Do I owe you something?

AARON   Stop it, will you?

Aaron turns his back. Traveler dives for his date book.

TRAVELER   Look, I'll pencil in Tuesday. If you decide you don't want to come, just let me know. (*He strikes a match. Aaron is observing him closely.*) My agent's on that phone. (*The Traveler points to the receiver, tries to light the half-smoked cigarette, is too nervous, gives up.*)

AARON (*quiet but concerned*)   How's your breathing?

The Traveler rolls his eyes, hating the question.

TRAVELER   I'm fine. (*pause*) I called Steiff.

AARON   What did he say?

TRAVELER (*uneasy*)   To go see him at the hospital if it gets worse.

AARON (*in an even voice*)   You want me to drive you up there now, just to check things out?

TRAVELER (*certain*)   No. (*He sips wine from the smudgy glass.*)

AARON   If you go, I want to go with you.

TRAVELER (*as if doing him a favor*)   All right. I'll call you. (*Dismissing the matter from his mind, he picks up the phone.*) Shit. She put me on hold. (*He hangs up.*) I hate "hold."

He gulps down the remaining coffee. Aaron, obviously familiar with the apartment, is quietly straightening up. He glances at the crumpled review.

It's the end of humans. We're turning into phones. McLuhan, Orwell, Huxley: they all say that—because it's true. (*As if to illustrate, he records a message on his telephone machine, keeping his voice pleasant but making funny contorted angry faces while he does it.*) Hi, I'm out. Please leave your number, and I'll call you back as soon as I possibly can.

When he lifts his finger from the "record" button he makes a "raspberry" sound at the phone. Immediately, as if in response, the phone rings. He stares at it before commenting rapidly.

TRAVELER   It's the pit cooling the cattle black.

AARON   What?

TRAVELER   It's . . . something . . . Wait. (*He holds his old flute, calming himself, then repeats slowly what he had intended to say.*) It's the pot calling the kettle black. (*Satisfied, he picks up speed again, grabbing for the phone and for food at the same time.*) Hi. (*As soon as he hears who it is, he silently screams, "No, no, no!" and bangs his fist on the table without actually hitting it.*)

TRAVELER   (*covering the receiver, mouthing to Aaron*)   It's my sister.

He rolls his eyes to indicate frustration. Aaron watches, concerned at his state of tension. The Traveler forces some enthusiasm into his voice as he speaks into the phone.

TRAVELER   Hi, Jodie. (*His hands scramble on his table for things to eat or drink.*) 'Course it's me. Yeah, I'm fine, I'm fine. Look, I can't talk. But I'm fine. I'm really fine.

Aaron picks up papers from the floor, still watching the Traveler carefully.

I'm out of breath because I've got a meeting. It's been a long day. Just work—a lot of things. You know—the opera, phone calls—this is New York, not Minneapolis. I'm fine. (*His voice crescendoes.*) I'm fine. I'm telling you—I'm fine! I'm fine! I'm fine—good-bye.

The Traveler looks confused. He has been trying to ignore his symptoms of heart failure: fluid in the lungs, and difficulty breathing. Now he's run out of steam. He feels like he's drowning. He's experiencing a slowdown of the world, as if the brakes had been slammed on. He totters, dizzy. Aaron, moving quickly, catches and supports him. As the apartment recedes from sight, an orderly enters with a hospital bed on wheels. He and Aaron help the Traveler onto the bed. They are now in a hospital room. The orderly removes the Traveler's sweatshirt and covers him with a sheet. Aaron stands by the bed, touching the Traveler. Jodie, the Traveler's sister, in her fifties, strong-looking, wearing browns and orange, stands by the bed too, holding the Traveler's tape recorder.

TRAVELER (*to Aaron*)   Drugs—when I wake up, I want to be drugged and distracted. There's nothing left to learn this time 'round.

JODIE (*solicitous*)   I told Doctor Steiff—

TRAVELER (*curtly*)   Jodie, please go. I'll be okay. See you later.

JODIE (*obediently*)   Okay. I'll have this fixed by then. (*Jodie is referring to the Traveler's tape recorder.*) See you in Recovery, kid. (*Jodie leaves.*)

TRAVELER (*to Aaron*)   Is she gone?

AARON   Yes.

The Traveler, hiding his head under the sheet, cries. Aaron cradles him. The Traveler stops crying.

TRAVELER   I'm not afraid of death. It's not that.

AARON   The pain?

TRAVELER   It'll be agony. For the third time. But it's familiar and it ends.

AARON   So what is it?

242

TRAVELER (*almost crying again*)   I'm afraid of living . . . diminished.

AARON   That's not in the cards, baby. No doctor ever said it was—

ORDERLY (*starting to push the bed*)   We got an appointment.

AARON (*walking alongside the cart*)   Are you feeling high yet?

TRAVELER   No. Listen, what if I'm awake, and I can't tell them? (*The Traveler shouts.*) Drugs!

AARON (*encouraging his spirit*)   That's it. Keep yelling!

TRAVELER (*still shouting*)   More drugs!

The orderly pushes the cart faster. Aaron is left behind in the dark. The Traveler shouts from his King Lear *opera as his cart is spun in circles around the stage by the orderly.*

TRAVELER (*shouting*)   "Blow, ye winds, and crack your cheeks.
Rage, blow, you cataracts and hurricanoes,
Spout 'til you've drenched our steeples, drowned the cocks,
You sulphurous thought-executing fires,
Vaunt-couriers to oak-cleaving thunderbolts . . ."

This moment marks a crossing from one state of the Traveler's mind to another. The bed with the Traveler stops in the operating area. The Traveler continues in a distorted way to be aware of what is happening. He lies on his bed facing upstage, his head tilted down and backward toward us. Three medical people—a woman doctor, an older male doctor and a younger male doctor—wearing green surgical gloves and robes, perform slow emblematic gestures. They don't hover over the patient. Checking their monitors, they are suddenly alarmed. Sound of a rapid beat.

WOMAN DOCTOR   No! (*The doctors adjust dials. The heartbeat sound normalizes. The crisis is over. She speaks more quietly.*) Oh, no.

YOUNGER MALE DOCTOR (*cool, continuing his work*)   Calm down.

OLDER MALE DOCTOR   We can't do anything about it now.

WOMAN DOCTOR   How damaged is he?

OLDER MALE DOCTOR   First things first. We operate. He wants to
live, doesn't he?

We hear what the Traveler desperately wants to scream.

TRAVELER'S VOICE (*screaming*)   No! Not like that!

*But the Traveler himself, whose face we see upside down, can't get any
sounds out at all. As he receives an injection of anesthesia: a single loud
sour sound of a Tibetan horn. The Traveler has entered an Inferno world of
surgery visions, a profound dream state. The music we hear is as if written
by the Traveler for his musical Manhattan Inferno. The percussive
rhythms are related to heartbeat and breathing. Some instruments used
include drums, horns and the deep human male voice. This is music in the
Tibetan manner, intended to awaken the soul to its demons. The Traveler
slips off his cart and wanders as if lost in a wood. Sound of wind.*

TRAVELER   Path lost.

*From now on, as a result of his stroke, when the Traveler is alone, he
speaks with the degree of facility, or lack of it, that he has at the end of the
play. His speech sounds clipped, as if he had a slight British accent, but he
does not speak like a deaf person, nor does he stutter more than indicated in
the text. He has little muscular difficulty forming words. But some of his
sounds are not real words, and he hears other people as if they were
speaking an unknown language.*

> Forest—again. Dark wood.
> Look to right, look to left.

*We hear a voice singing a song the Traveler wrote. The Traveler mouths
the words.*

VOICE SINGING   In the middle of the path of life
> I lost my way.
> In the middle of the path of life
> I lost my way,
> And found myself in shadows.

I found myself in a forest,
And in the forest, it was night.
In the forest it was cold,
And I tremble now to speak of it,
And feel close to dying.

TRAVELER   Looking to right, to left, to guide.
To living? To dead?
You never think about some place like earth.

Inferno souls appear, embodying disconnected shadows and reflections of the Traveler's life. They are clothed in soft dark material which also covers their faces.

LOUDSPEAKER (*impersonal hospital voice*)   Open heart. Open heart.

TRAVELER   Five years old: rheum-a-tic fever.

The Traveler watches as the Inferno souls pull a small boy strapped to a wheeled cart.

My-self. It's true.

The souls and the Traveler paddle the operating bed as if it were a boat crossing a wide dangerous river.

Now wa-ter. Only wa-ter—not stop, not stop.
To left, to right, to right, to left—not stop, not stop.

The souls become children playing in slow motion, with accompanying playground sounds.

TRAVELER   It's ten. Ten years old—again rheum-a-tic.
It's Children's Cardiac Home.
To right, to left—not stop, not stop.

A childlike voice sings a song from the Traveler's unfinished opera of King Lear. *The song sounds medieval, but also teasing.*

CHILDLIKE VOICE (*singing*)   "Have more than you show,
Speak less than you know,
Lend less than you owe . . ."

TRAVELER   It's Children's Cardiac Home.
It's Monday—playing wedding to child wife.

The souls and the Traveler enact a play wedding at the Children's Cardiac Home. The Traveler plays the groom.

To right, to left—not stop, not stop.
It's Tuesday: child wife choosing to left.

The child wife dies. The Traveler and the souls continue to paddle, as if afraid that if they stop they too will die.

Good-bye, good-bye. Not stop, not stop.

CHILDLIKE VOICE (*singing*)   "The sweet and bitter fool will presently appear;
The one in motley here, the other found out there."

TRAVELER   To left, to right. To right, to left. Not stop, not stop.
Good-bye, good-bye.
It's twelve. My-self to family again.
It's new city: Minipolice, Minn-e-so-tta.

A shopping cart is wheeled around the stage, with Jodie kneeling in it.

TRAVELER   Looking to friend to right, to left.
Not trust family. Only my-self—
Not stop, not stop. To left, to right . . .

The drumming is faster.

It's twenty. It's beau-tiful New York.

The souls pose as perfect beautiful people in ads.

Twenty: myself sick again. It's New York.
Shhh. Shhh. New York: "sick," it's secret.

The souls dance in slow motion, hands tied behind them.

Twisting—like city—like that.

The souls move slowly as the drum beats fast. The Traveler is attracted to what the souls seem to have: power, sexuality, immunity to pain, beauty . . .

246

Circling to cars, looking to eyes—
To fuckings, to druggings, to buyings things, to rest-aurants—
Not stop, not stop.
To alc-o-hols—not stop, not stop.
Sometimes many. Always alone.

The souls leave the Traveler alone on stage.

LOUDSPEAKER   Open heart. Open heart.

The Traveler must decide whether to live or die, symbolized by taking the right or left path.

TRAVELER   Myself to right? To left? To dead? To left?
To living? To right? To light, to right?
To resting, to left?
Must my-self choosing.
Choosing to right, to light. Coming to light.

With this commitment, a different light begins to dawn.

TRAVELER   My-self choosing to right. Feeling like that. My-self to right.

The Traveler stands on his hospital bed, arms outstretched, experiencing himself as if out in the cosmos in a state of innocence. Music changes to Ravel's piano concerto.

Like baby. Like angel. Feeling like that.
Like traveling to stars, to friends.
Beginning. Beginning like baby.
Before walking. Before talking. Before thinking. It's different.
To stars looking to earth. It's wonderful really. It's true.
To stars. Like angel. Looking to earth.

The Traveler, standing on his bed, as if out in sunshine, hears a new and haunting phrase of music, quite simple. Later in the play he will try to recall it, to use it as the melody in a new composition. Aaron, in a waiting room, in his mind speaks as if to the Traveler—trying to communicate calm to him.

AARON (*softly*)   You're in a clean meadow
In sunlight, lying on a hill.
Your will is strong. Your body's strong.
Listen to the wind rustling in the birch leaves.
Listen to the bees.

LOUDSPEAKER   Open heart. Open heart.

TRAVELER   Looking to earth. Like baby.
Difficult . . . to born.

He sits on the bed again.

Must to born.

The light changes. The Traveler lies back down on the operating bed. He is bandaged. Jodie comes over to Aaron. Working on the Traveler's tape recorder has been her way of helping with the operation.

JODIE (*waving the tape recorder, triumphant*)   It works! I've fixed it!

Dr. Steiff, the cardiologist, enters the waiting area to speak to Jodie and Aaron. Steiff is not identifiable as one of the doctors who administered the anesthetic. Steiff looks bland and tired. He always speaks in an even tone.

DR. STEIFF   Well, his heart responded beautifully. He's off the heart-lung machine. There were no surgical complications. The new valve is in and working fine.

AARON (*softly, moved*)   He did it.

Aaron turns to hug Jodie, who turns toward the doctor.

JODIE (*effusively grateful*)   Thank you, Doctor, thank you.

AARON (*to Steiff*)   When may we see him?

DR. STEIFF (*glancing at his watch*)   They're sewing him up now.
That'll take a while. Then he'll be wheeled to open heart recovery. The time to get him hooked up and monitored down.

Steiff leaves. Jodie and Aaron leave together. As the Traveler is wheeled to the cardiac recovery room, the music is muted, gentle and funny—music for a newborn. A nurse and an orderly seem to slowly and softly fly around the rolling bed like birds. The Traveler, though still drugged, is now a little more conscious but dazed and weak, like a baby.

TRAVELER (*in wonderment*)   Beginning to born. Billions to stars . . .
to planets . . .
Only one earth—it's sad.
Awake—it's funny.

A nurse enters the Traveler's line of vision, hopping by like a kangaroo. The Traveler comments to the audience as if to a friend.

Seeing like that. True.

The nurse's behavior returns to hospital reality.

Not true really. Seeing like that.

A phone rings. Laurie, another nurse, answers it.

LAURIE (*lewdly*)   Open heart, hello.

We have heard her as the Traveler has heard her in his altered state. Then she is back in hospital reality.

TRAVELER   "Open heart, hello." Not real—real.

Jodie and Aaron are led by Dr. Steiff to the Traveler's bedside.

DR. STEIFF (*speaking unnecessarily loudly to the Traveler*)   You're in the recovery room. Your operation went fine. Everything went fine. (*He speaks to Aaron and Jodie.*) He may or may not hear you.

TRAVELER (*to himself*)   Myself hear. It's true.

Dr. Steiff, seen through the Traveler's eyes, suddenly whinnies and paws the ground like a horse.

Funny—like horse.

Steiff's behavior is appropriate again to hospital reality.

AARON (*to the Traveler, taking his hand*)   You did it. It's over.

JODIE (*speaking loudly into the Traveler's ear*)   It's Jodie. Jodie. I'll be here to see you every day. I called Lily in Minneapolis. Lily is sending Paul—her son Paul. Can you hear me, kid? It's Jodie.

LAURIE (*efficiently herding Jodie and Aaron out*)   You can see him tomorrow.

TRAVELER (*alone, softly, to himself*)   Myself want say: "Terrible the tube.
Throat hurt. Thirsty."
Cannot—because tube.
Myself anger, like lightning to bomb—
Heart cut. Again.
Why cut? Why curse to *my*-self?

The Traveler gradually becomes agitated. We hear a slow warning beeper sound.

Thirty—to cut heart first time: forest, dark wood.
Thir-ty-six it's again—to cut. Again forest. Now again dead.
Middle my life—*to cut.*
It's knife—knife and *to cut.*
Three time *to cut.* It's curse.
Myself see Jodie. Angry to Jodie. Hate to family.
Angry to fate. Hate to God.

The Traveler is agitated now, although still very weak.

To left, to left, to left!

The warning beeper has become rapid. The nurses adjust dials and pour medicine into the Traveler's intravenous tube. The Traveler deliberately sets out to calm himself.

Can-not to left.
Choose to right,
To quiet: must my-self to quiet, to thinking—to quiet.

He has quieted himself. Laurie checks his pulse against her watch. The Traveler, observing this, decides to quiet himself further by thinking about an abstract topic: time.

Thinking now to "time."

This moment is stretched out aurally by bell-like reverberations, and visually by the slowed-down actions of the nurses.

"Time"—it's different now.
Every second coming to changing.

Back to usual hospital reality. The Traveler describes what he is feeling as he feels it. Since waking from the operation, he has a quality of innocence, of being surprised by every feeling.

Feeling now—it's different—
It's—intense.
That's word: "intense." Wow.
Every minute: "intense."
It's changing. Intense again—wow.
Every minute changing like that. It's funny.
Minute feeling like day. Day to thousand year. Feeling like that.
Maybe million year before "to cut,"
Maybe million after . . . Myself not knowing.

Within the Traveler's line of vision a male nurse hops like a kangaroo.

Like kanga—like roo. Roo. Zoo. Roozoo.

Back to hospital reality. Laurie adjusts the bed so the Traveler can sit more comfortably.

LAURIE (*to the Traveler, as he hears her*)   Share. Shash mush me nore momargible.

TRAVELER (*to himself*)   Myself not German. Only English. (*He tries to tell Laurie he speaks English, not German.*) Shalef nosh shaman. Ponly shingle.

The nurses look at each other. The Traveler does not yet realize he sounds as foreign to others as they sound to him.

LAURIE (*to the male nurse*)   Maybe the anesthetic. But call Doctor Steiff.

TRAVELER (*to himself*)   Waking up—it's mysterious.
Wanting lovers—every everyones.
It's true—feeling like that.

Laurie, as seen by the Traveler, is posing suggestively by the bed. The phone rings. The Traveler watches the male nurse answer it.

MALE NURSE (*answering the phone, posing suggestively*)   Open heart, hello.

Back to hospital reality. Laurie helps the Traveler sit up.

LAURIE   Easy. Easy. That's it. (*She hands him a plastic cup with a bent straw in it.*) See if you can hold this.

The Traveler has trouble grasping with his right hand.

No? How about your left hand? (*She puts the cup in his left hand.*) Good.

She makes a note in her records. The male nurse ushers Jodie toward the Traveler's bed.

MALE NURSE (*to the Traveler*)   Your sister's here.

JODIE (*full of energy*)   Hi, kid. Sitting on your first day—that's great. (*She reads Laurie's name on her badge.*) Laurie here says you're doing fine. (*to Laurie*) Shall we call you Laurie?

LAURIE   Sure.

JODIE (*shaking Laurie's hand*)   I'm Jodie. This is his third time 'round, Laurie. We're veterans. He's sitting up already. That's great.

LAURIE   We've speeded up our system here. And your brother's a strong man.

JODIE (*to the Traveler*)   So, how are you feeling?

TRAVELER (*using the only real word he can*)   Yeah.

JODIE   Okay?

TRAVELER   Shashloman shasha.

JODIE   Does it hurt? Your chest?

TRAVELER   Shushuh to left, shashlahmon, yeah to left.

JODIE   What'd you say? It hurts on the left?

Jodie points to the Traveler's left side. The Traveler understands this question.

TRAVELER *(meaning to say "no")*   Yeah.

JODIE *(to Laurie)*   He says it hurts on the left. Can we have more painkiller, Laurie?

LAURIE   He's high as a kite now.

It looks to the Traveler as if Jodie's pointing finger is going suggestively into Laurie's open mouth. Then Jodie's behavior is back to hospital reality.

JODIE   Lily is sending Paul from Minneapolis to see you.

TRAVELER   Shaashla shashba amashaba.

JODIE *(to Laurie)*   What's wrong with the way he's speaking?

TRAVELER *(to himself)*   It's to Sweden?

LAURIE   We've reported it.

JODIE   Should we worry about it, Laurie?

LAURIE   Might be the anesthetic.

JODIE *(to the Traveler)*   Laurie says: "Don't worry. It's the anesthetic."

The Traveler is finished with the orange juice. Jodie takes the glass from him.

JODIE *(pronouncing her words carefully)*   Can you understand what I'm saying?

TRAVELER *(not understanding)*   Shashplash, yeah.

253

JODIE (*hopefully*) That's good.

TRAVELER (*having no clue as to what she's just said*) Yeah.

LAURIE (*briskly lowering the Traveler's bed*) Okay, Jodie. Come back later. He's tired.

Aaron enters the recovery room. He has brought the Traveler his old wooden flute. He hands it to him.

AARON (*upset, to Laurie*) Where is Steiff?

LAURIE (*avoiding Aaron's gaze*) I don't know.

The lights dim on the recovery room as Aaron pulls Jodie out into the corridor.

AARON (*certain*) It's a *stroke!*

JODIE Don't you dare tell people my brother's had a—that.

AARON (*forcing himself to use the word again*) A stroke!

JODIE Are you a medical authority?

AARON Jodie, it's obvious.

JODIE Doctor Steiff did *not* say that!

AARON He can't—

JODIE He did *not* use that word.

AARON He can't—but it's a stroke. I can't think in here. It's too stuffy. Come on outside. Let's get some fresh air.

JODIE You get some fresh air! I'm sitting right here, right here—in case I'm needed.

Jodie remains seated like a soldier, staring straight ahead. Aaron runs out, anguished. Music: dancelike and joyous—something between a Bach fugue and a Nino Rota score for a Fellini film. The Traveler, still feeling euphoric from the drugs, on his hospital bed and still attached to an IV bottle, is wheeled by an orderly through corridors from the recovery room to his room.

People smile and wave at him. He is accompanied by Moira, a private duty nurse carrying the medical records; by Jodie, carrying the tape recorder; and by Aaron, carrying red flowers. In the Traveler's eyes, everyone's actions seem disconnected and repeated: flowers are passed under his nose, an orderly spills a bedpan and cleans up, the bed weaves this way and that. Then the music stops and the Traveler is left alone in his room.

TRAVELER (*alone, to himself*) Wow. Foreign to exile. Feeling like that.
Exile to earth. It's true.
Like baby . . . to earth . . .

This train of thought leads him to remembering the phrase of melody he heard during the operation.

It's song.

He reaches with his left hand for his wooden flute. He tries to play it. What comes out sounds like nothing. He swings his left arm back and forth. He tries to sing the notes of the melody, but that doesn't come out right either. His sound crescendoes into a scream of frustration and rage.

TRAVELER Ahhhhhhhhhhhhhhh . . .

Aaron comes in with Moira, and touches the Traveler to reassure him. Moira makes sure nothing is physically wrong.

MOIRA What was that? You have a powerful voice. You really do. I don't think there's much fluid in *your* lungs.

She takes his pulse. Out of his carryall bag, Aaron pulls the Traveler's bathrobe, vitamin bottles and fruit. He hangs up the bathrobe, arranges the vitamins and fruit on the night table.

MOIRA (*to Aaron*) Is he a singer too?

AARON No, a composer.

MOIRA (*not paying attention, leaving*) Lovely.

The Traveler waves away the pile of cards, letters and telegrams Aaron has in his hand.

AARON (*getting it from his bag, showing it to the Traveler*) Look, I brought your shaving brush.

TRAVELER (*meaning to say "brush"*) Klipklop.

AARON Brush. (*He writes it down for the Traveler.*) Can you read it?

TRAVELER (*trying*) Cramplow. Shash. (*He has a sudden change of mood.*) Amblashtrahsh wablash . . .

The Traveler is trying to tell the story of what happened when he was being given anesthesia, the stroke moment. Without much affect, the Traveler mimics the panic of the woman doctor.

Washasha. Ahhhh. Ahhhh.

AARON I'm sorry. I don't get it.

TRAVELER Ashmash. Ahhhh.

AARON (*as if guessing a charade*) Someone in pain?

TRAVELER (*still trying to mimic the woman doctor*) Ahhh. Ahhh. Grashmashah. Ahhh.

AARON In the recovery room?

TRAVELER (*stabbing in the dark*) Yeah.

AARON (*not sure he's understood*) Was it in the recovery room?

The Traveler looks doubtful.

AARON Was it a man?

Not understanding the question, the Traveler has dropped the story and is listlessly staring into space.

TRAVELER Yeah.

AARON (*realizing that the Traveler's response was inappropriate*) Was it a woman?

TRAVELER (*looking blank*) Yeah.

A young intern comes in with a tourniquet and a needle to take some blood.

INTERN (*going right to work, but nervous*)   Hello.

TRAVELER   Hi.

INTERN   How we doing? Been following the game?

Aaron holds the Traveler's other hand, which the Traveler squeezes hard. When the needle goes in, both the Traveler and Aaron wince. The intern has missed the vein.

INTERN (*muttering*)   Sorry. (*The intern tries to remain jolly.*) Well, if at once you don't succeed—right?

Once more the intern plunges in. This time the Traveler and Aaron make no sound.

INTERN (*flustered*)   Sorry. (*The intern, increasingly nervous, has missed again.*) We'll get it this time.

This time when the intern stabs, both the Traveler and Aaron scream. The intern glances at them, unnerved. He has drawn blood. Dr. Steiff watches the end of this performance from the door of the Traveler's room.

INTERN   Okay. We'll use the other arm tomorrow.

DR. STEIFF (*taking the Traveler's chart from the intern as he leaves*)   We'll just do that every other day now.

The Traveler watches Steiff intently. The doctor is obviously important to him.

TRAVELER   Hi.

DR. STEIFF   Hi.

Dr. Steiff appears to paw the ground and whinny like a horse. Then, back to normal, he sits on the bed. Aaron remains standing. Dr. Steiff addresses the Traveler as if he can understand every word.

DR. STEIFF   Cardiologically, I see no complications whatever. You must be getting used to these heart operations.

TRAVELER Shasha folah . . .

DR. STEIFF (*as if the Traveler had asked the question*) You can have a second sleeping pill, although I gather you've been sleeping fine. (*to Aaron*) I don't think he needs the night nurse anymore. (*to the Traveler*) I hear you brushed your teeth with soap this morning. That's the sort of thing we want to polish up before you leave. I mean—

Though he understands little of what Dr. Steiff is saying, the Traveler is paying close attention to him, playacting well the attitude of a patient listening to his doctor.

TRAVELER Shahsh shershash shh—?

DR. STEIFF (*cool as a cucumber, responding as if he understood the Traveler perfectly*) The speech therapist is on vacation. She'll be back Tuesday.

TRAVELER Sher . . . Shahsh . . . ? (*Needing help, he glances at Aaron.*)

AARON (*straightforwardly asking what he perceives to be the Traveler's question*) How long will this speech thing last?

DR. STEIFF (*to the Traveler*) We need more tests to determine which part of the brain is affected. Let me see you move your leg. (*He touches the Traveler's right leg. The Traveler touches it too.*) Fine. Anything else?

Dr. Steiff, about to leave, again whinnies and paws like a horse. The Traveler glances at Aaron to see if he saw what he did. Aaron did not.

TRAVELER (*meaning good-bye*) Hi.

DR. STEIFF (*casually*) So long. (*He leaves.*)

AARON Did you understand him? You acted like you did, but . . .

TRAVELER (*momentarily articulate with emotion*) Baby, what are we going to do?

258

Aaron is amazed and moved. They hold each other.

AARON   We'll be okay. We'll be okay. I promise—we'll be okay.

TRAVELER   Gash mash good-bye, good-bye . . . okay . . . to left
. . . okay . . . sayswash good-bye, good-bye . . . sayswash . . .

AARON (*speaking powerfully, understanding that the Traveler is talking of
suicide*)   No. *Not* "good-bye, good-bye."

TRAVELER   Sayswash?

AARON (*suddenly guessing correctly*)   I get it! You want to know how
your heart is!

Aaron demonstrates a heart beating. The Traveler watches Aaron intently.

Your heart's okay now. It's completely okay.

*Aaron is learning that it helps to speak to the Traveler with much expression
in his voice. The Traveler gestures something which refers to the intern's
taking blood.*

What? The injection? More painkiller? You can't. You'll get
hooked. (*Aaron realizes he's on the wrong track.*) No. Damn. But
it's to do with a needle, yes?

TRAVELER (*trying to say "needle"*)   Yeah: lusin. Lusin. Yeah.

AARON (*frustrated*)   I'm sorry. I don't understand. Damn. Damn.
Damn.

The Traveler, frustrated too, throws the shaving brush across the room.

Wait. Wait. Hold it. (*Aaron focuses his attention.*) We can't both
lose it. Come on, Aaron, you're good at charades. (*He gets it.*)
Needle . . . The blood! What an airhead! (*He hits himself.*) You
don't know *why* they're taking blood, do you? Blood? (*He mimes
the intern taking blood.*)

TRAVELER (*that's it*)   Shlash. Mashlash right.

AARON   Okay. Nada problema. The new valve is okay. A great
valve. Beautiful piece of sculpture. But it's *metal.* (*He knocks on*

something metal.) And for a metal valve— (*He knocks on metal again.*) —the blood has to be not too thin, not too thick.

Aaron accompanies the words "thick" and "thin" with signs. He is discovering that when he simultaneously speaks and makes an appropriate gesture, the Traveler understands better. The Traveler listens carefully. From Aaron's tone of voice as much as from his words, eventually the Traveler understands.

So they check the blood. But there's nothing wrong with your heart now. Your heart is A-OK. Okay. This metal valve will last for years and years and years. (*He speaks in a progressively older voice.*) You'll live to be eighty, ninety, a hundred years old.

TRAVELER (*getting it*)   Hushray o'clock? Yeah?

AARON (*pretending to be very old*)   You'll live to be an old, old man.

TRAVELER (*greatly relieved*)   Yeah? No kidding?

AARON   No kidding.

TRAVELER   Wow!

AARON   We did it—hooray! (*Aaron falls to the floor in happy exhaustion.*) Whew!

TRAVELER (*with effort, saying thanks*)   You're . . . okay.

AARON (*amazed the Traveler has said that*)   Wow. That's the nicest thing you've ever said to me. You're okay too. (*Aaron hops up on the bed, sits beside the Traveler.*) It's weird. I feel like—everything's fine now. Better than before. Is it terrible to feel that way?

EKG LADY (*at the door*)   I'm here to take his EKG.

AARON (*getting off the bed, to the Traveler*)   You want me to get ice cream? Ice cream? "You scream, They scream, We all scream for ice cream"?

He's not understanding. Aaron hits his forehead as if he were spastic, missing his mouth with an ice cream cone.

TRAVELER (*his face lighting up*)   Yeah. Wow.

Aaron throws him a kiss, leaves happily. The EKG technician does her work. As she speaks, the Traveler sees her transform into a dog.

EKG LADY (*barking*)   Not much room here.

TRAVELER (*asking about EKG results*)   Grash shamal?

EKG LADY (*barking again*)   It's your pulse.

TRAVELER   Trash?

EKG LADY (*normal, matter-of-fact*)   Your pulse. Recording your heart pulsing.

TRAVELER (*to himself as the EKG lady, turning her back to him, winds up her work*)   Pulsing . . . Breathing. . . .
Humans' breathing—it's same to animal.
To animal, to human—exactly.
Coming to earth, it's feeling,
It's breathing, pulsing.
Earth: it's tiny.
Thinking like that. It's funny.

The Traveler picks up his old flute and tries again to play the melody he remembers from his surgery dreams. He can't. Moira comes in, accompanied by an orderly with a wheelchair. The Traveler focuses on exercising his right hand.

MOIRA   I'm going to make your bed. It's time to sit.

TRAVELER   Pellog?

MOIRA   Sit. It's time to sit. Now swing your legs 'round. Good. Hold on to me. Let your good hand take your weight. That's it. How's your other hand?

She takes his flute from him for a moment.

TRAVELER   Sha?

She and the orderly slip a bathrobe on the Traveler, then hand him back his flute.

MOIRA   It's getting better, isn't it? And the leg?

TRAVELER (*not understanding, making conversation*)   Sha, sha . . .

As Moira speaks to the Traveler, she and the orderly deftly swing the Traveler's legs over the side of the bed, stand him up, lean him forward onto the orderly's body. The orderly lets him down into the wheelchair, then moves the IV bottle from the bed to a stand on wheels and leaves. Moira puts the Traveler's slippers on his feet.

MOIRA (*conversationally*)   So we don't have to cut it off?

TRAVELER (*innocently making conversation too*)   Yeah, shalmashasha.

MOIRA   Oh, so you'd *like* to cut it off, would you?

TRAVELER (*not the vaguest idea what she's saying*)   Shashahshasha.

MOIRA   Shall we ask Surgeon to slice it off, then?

TRAVELER   Shashasha.

MOIRA   Get rid of it completely?

TRAVELER   Shasha . . .

MOIRA   Isn't that the best way?

TRAVELER (*making small talk*)   Sha, yeah . . .

MOIRA (*continuing her joke at the Traveler's expense*)   I think so. And the other leg? We'll have him take that one too, shall we?

TRAVELER (*irritated, understanding that he's being asked questions he can't answer*)   Yeah, yeah, yeah.

MOIRA (*having gotten him settled*)   Comfortable?

Moira hands the Traveler the remote wand for the TV. The TV monitor is high up, facing the Traveler but not the audience. Moira straightens the bed, then leaves. The Traveler watches TV. He hears words spoken as if in an unknown language, but the tones of voice are clear to him. The President is making a speech.

TRAVELER *(laughing, to himself)*   She's not true, pres-dent.

The Traveler imitates the President's falsely sincere tone. He comments on the President's speech.

> Smiley only to lips—never to eyes. Thinkin' 'bout that.
> Words myself nothing, of course—it's "tone."
> It's word: "tone."
> "Tone": it's "secret language." It's true.
> "Tone": it's "tune." "Tune." "Tune-tone": it's music.

He switches channels. We hear background music and sounds of dialogue, but no comprehensible words.

> Listening to face. Humans' face, it's wonderful—it's changing.
> Changing to eyes, to lips: it's true.
> It's "secret language." "Communication." Wow. It's word.
> Humans' face communication to me.

He channel-surfs, watching faces, mimicking them, the TV volume low. Jodie enters the Traveler's room.

JODIE   Hi. It's me.

The Traveler is engrossed in the TV.

> I have something to tell you.

Jodie turns down the volume on the TV. The Traveler is not pleased by this.

> Is it okay to tell you something?

Soap opera music from the TV at low volume.

TRAVELER   Shash?

Jodie, working herself up to what she wants to say, takes a drink of water from a table. She paces behind the Traveler's chair while the Traveler continues to watch television.

JODIE Last time I came to New York, you treated me like nothing. You know that? I just sat there in your apartment listening to you wheeling and dealing all the time on the phone. Coming and going, wheeling and dealing. There must have been a traffic jam in your head.

Jodie takes another drink. The Traveler sees this and indicates he would like some water too, but Jodie doesn't see his gesture.

Now it's different, right? You've got time for me in the hospital, right? And besides, you're feeling better, right?

TRAVELER (*saying whatever, watching the soap*) Trasha, trasha, trasha . . .

JODIE Yeah, what the hell, right? Remember, when you were thirteen—you told your friends I was the most boring person you'd ever met? Maybe you were right. So you were ashamed of me. My little brother. Who knew you'd turn out to be a star? I did. I knew. Did you know I was scared of you then?

Jodie, behind the wheelchair, reaches out to touch the Traveler's head, but withdraws her hand before touching it.

TRAVELER (*wanting water*) Wa . . . watergate. (*The Traveler is surprised to hear himself say this.*)

JODIE (*pacing behind the Traveler*) You think it's a Watergate? You and me? I don't. I mean, you were the baby and you were sick, so you got all the attention. So what? I was ripped off. So what? I mean I know I'm not a creative person. I know that. I'm boring, probably. Yeah, boring. So what?

TRAVELER (*still wanting water*) Yeah. Wantergate. (*The Traveler is surprised at this word coming out too.*)

JODIE So we're family. That's what. Family. That what counts. You live alone, I live alone. So, why should we live alone?

TRAVELER "Wantergate"?

Jodie comes to the Traveler's side. She turns off the TV.

JODIE (*nervous about how her idea will go down*)   So, listen—you'll come, you'll come live with me now—in Minneapolis? Right? Minneapolis? Why not, right? We're family.

The Traveler understands the word "Minneapolis."

TRAVELER (*not pleased*)   Mini . . . police?

JODIE (*sweating it out*)   Yeah, I mean we could buy a, a house together. How about that?

The Traveler looks angry.

TRAVELER (*furious but unable to say "no"*)   Mini!

MOIRA (*knocking, speaking from the door*)   He has a visitor.

JODIE (*glad the confrontation is postponed*)   Okay, just think about it. Okay? You don't have to tell me now. Just think about it, okay? (*Jodie backs out the door, bumping into Moira.*) Sorry. (*She is gone.*)

MOIRA (*to the Traveler*)   Your nephew. Paul.

TRAVELER (*not understanding*)   Shasha?

Moira leaves. The Traveler maneuvers his wheelchair to the water pitcher, has difficulty pouring the water. Paul enters the room. He's young, open and intelligent-looking. He pours water into the glass for the Traveler, who drinks without looking to see who helped him.

TRAVELER (*not looking up, saying "thanks"*)   Hi.

PAUL   Hi.

The Traveler recognizes Paul's voice. He looks up.

TRAVELER (*delighted*)   Hi!

Paul kisses him. The Traveler touches Paul, who remains kneeling by the wheelchair. They both realize that the Traveler is not understanding every word Paul says, but it doesn't matter to them.

PAUL   Hi. I'm really glad to see you.

TRAVELER (*lovingly*)   Yeah . . . mosha . . .

PAUL I brought you this. (*Unwrapping it carefully, he shows the Traveler a beautiful Native American rattle.*) I got it from a Sioux medicine man. It's a power wand. (*He hands it to the Traveler, who holds it.*) You're supposed to shake it gently. (*With his hand over the Traveler's, Paul gives the wand a gentle shake. Then the Traveler shakes it alone.*)

TRAVELER Yeah.

PAUL So look, when are we going to sing together again? I don't want to be the only musician in the family for long, you know.

TRAVELER Yeah . . .

The Traveler shakes the rattle, shouting a little, and the energy of this gets him standing, leaning on Paul. Paul puts his arm around the Traveler's waist to steady him. Moira appears.

TRAVELER Hi.

Moira has nothing to say. Leaning on Paul, the Traveler walks slowly, with determination and effort. Music. His right side—including his hand— is contracted, his right leg is weak and his right foot has a tendency to drag.

TRAVELER (*as he walks*) To right, to left . . .
Body to right, head to left. Body to left, head to right.
Sometimes understand. Sometimes nothing.

Time is passing. The Traveler eventually walks by himself, leaning on the rolling IV stand. He is feeling paranoid, and the people in the hospital corridor appear to him to be hostile.

Looking to right, to left. Looking to eyes.
Not earth, not hell . . . Corridor to hospital, it's Purgation.
Body to left, head to right.
Everybodys to looking.
See me. See me where?
Hospital for born, for dying—that's all.
Looking to friend to left, to right.

Aaron, carrying his bag, joins him walking, takes his arm. The people in the corridor assume a more usual aspect. Days pass and the Traveler is walking with less difficulty, although his right leg is still not under control, his right hand remains stiff and he looks fragile. Another patient, passing in a wheelchair, nods.

PATIENT Hello.

TRAVELER Hi.

PATIENT Out for a stroll?

TRAVELER Yeah, okay.

The patient, smiling, has gone. The walking music stops. Aaron conspiratorially pokes his elbow into the Traveler's side.

AARON You passed! You did it.

The Traveler is pleased. Then, in an abrupt mood change, he becomes sad.

TRAVELER Shasolashashh because shamer.

They've reached the solarium. The Traveler sits.

Downshashit.

AARON (*sitting next to him, an arm around his shoulder*) Feeling down like shit?

TRAVELER (*getting out exactly what he means*) *Visi d'arte.*

AARON (*amazed he has said this*) *Visi d'arte? Visi d'arte Tosca?* I live for art?

The Traveler extracts an audio tape from the pocket of his bathrobe, hands it to Aaron.

TRAVELER (*trying to say it again*) Griming . . . guy . . .

Aaron pulls the Traveler's tape machine from his bag and inserts the tape of Leontyne Price singing Visi d'Arte *from* Tosca. *They listen, sitting close together. The Traveler sobs quietly as he tells Aaron about the terrible things that have happened in his life, and how unfair it is. Most of his words are unintelligible. Aaron encourages him, holds him.*

TRAVELER   Five, to ten. Asha. To asha. Because shaasha. Ahh. Ahhh. Shashah. Shahshah. Ashashah. Shaa Mashash. To left. Shahah shah . . .

AARON (*murmuring, not interrupting the Traveler*)   I know, I know . . .

TRAVELER   Tasham shamash shash shash to right to left. Shash. Again. Again.

AARON (*as the Traveler speaks*)   I know . . . you've been so brave . . . you've came so close to dying . . . again and again . . .

TRAVELER   Ashashmash. Ten thousand years. Shamash. Shamash. Shamash . . . Shamash. Again. Because again. Again! Shamash. Ahhh, ahhh. Shaaamash maaaaaaaaash . . .

Aaron rocks him. The Traveler quiets down. The aria is over. Lightning is visible outside the window.

AARON (*to distract the Traveler*)   Look. It's a summer storm. Storm.

Aaron directs the Traveler's attention to the window. The Traveler walks downstage to look, interested.

TRAVELER (*to himself*)   Storm. It's word: "storm." Wow. Saying "storm," feeling "storm." It's true: word—it's feeling. Feeling— it's "intense." It's changing. Like storm to wind. Wow—"wind!" It's word. Every minute changing—whew! It's "storm." It's "wind."

Aaron comes down to the Traveler. The Traveler speaks softly because he cannot do otherwise.

Crash, fash, crash pash pash mash!
Pash! Crash! Plash flashpash crash!
Mashafalash, prash,
Pash pash cash prash pash pashpash, frash,
Fash shash.

AARON   Cadences—you're speaking in cadences! Go on.

TRAVELER   Pash pashposhfush cash tash-mashpushpash pashash—

AARON A song?

TRAVELER Mash-mashash tash hash-blahash flashlash—
Frash pash mash whaash hash!

The Traveler indicates a long beard.

AARON (*He's got it.*) *Lear!* Your opera—Lear on the heath!

TRAVELER Flash mash—

AARON (*expressing the Traveler's defiance more energetically than the Traveler can himself*) Rage, blow—

TRAVELER Crash flash, mash hash kash plash—

AARON (*speaking at a volume the Traveler can't*) "Blow, winds, and crack your cheeks!"

TRAVELER Pash! Mash!

AARON "Rage! Blow!"

TRAVELER . . . Pash flappermash mash pashimashmo . . .

AARON ". . . You cataracts and hurricanoes . . ."

TRAVELER Spash, pee too vash drashed ash shlaffash—

AARON (*not remembering all the words*) Spash pee too vash drashed ash shlaffash—"Spout 'til you've drenched our steeples . . ."

TRAVELER . . . frashed ash cash!

AARON (*laughing*) ". . . drowned our cocks!"

TRAVELER (*turning to Aaron*) Shash, fow!

AARON (*swinging the Traveler's arm in the air*) Rage, blow!

They are both exhilarated. Lights out. Intermission.

ACT TWO

A few days later. The Traveler, wearing his own comfortable sweatpants and sweatshirt, is alone in the solarium in a wheelchair, playing with his tape machine.

DR. SULLIVAN (*standing still at the entrance to the solarium*) Excuse me. Mr. Moses?

Dr. Sullivan is young, quiet and attractive. A healing calm seems to radiate effortlessly from her. She shakes hands with the Traveler, kneels by him.

DR. SULLIVAN (*to the Traveler*) Mr. Moses, I'm Tina Sullivan from Rehab. I'm a fan. It's an honor to meet you. I saw your Dante piece twice. I loved it. You're coming to Rehab in a few days, so we need to make a quick evaluation.

Her questions are spoken clearly, without patronization.

Mr. Moses, can you understand what I'm saying?

TRAVELER (*knowing she's asking a question*) Yeah.

DR. SULLIVAN (*calmly*) That's good. I'm going to ask you some questions. Please answer "yes" or "no." (*She holds up a pen.*) Do you know what this is?

TRAVELER (*using his main word*) Yeah . . .

DR. SULLIVAN What is the name of this object?

TRAVELER Yeah.

She holds up her hand with no pen in it.

DR. SULLIVAN Am I still holding a pen?

TRAVELER Yeah. Blasha.

DR. SULLIVAN Can you say the word "no"?

TRAVELER Yeah.

DR. SULLIVAN   Will you say it for me, please?

TRAVELER   Okay.

Dr. Sullivan takes matches, a candle and an ashtray from her purse. She places these on her clipboard.

DR. SULLIVAN (*still clear and calm*)   There are three objects here: an ashtray, a candle, and matches. (*She puts the clipboard on the Traveler's lap.*) Would you put the matches in the ashtray, please?

The Traveler looks at her quizzically. Dr. Sullivan indicates the group of objects. The Traveler strikes a match, with which he carefully lights the candle. He is pleased at having done what he guessed was asked of him.

DR. SULLIVAN (*not changing her tone*)   Thank you, Mr. Moses. I don't need to examine your hand or your leg. They're coming along. I'm glad to have met you.

TRAVELER (*cordially*)   Yeah. Hi.

DR. SULLIVAN   See you in Rehab in a few days. (*Dr. Sullivan leaves.*)

TRAVELER (*in a good mood, to himself*)   Feeling like Mickey. Myself to Mickey. (*He laughs, plays with the word.*) Mickey. Mickey, Mickey.

Paul enters the solarium holding an audio tape.

PAUL   Hi.

TRAVELER (*to Paul, still playing with the word*)   Micking. Licking.

PAUL (*jumping into the game*)   Yeah? Licking?

TRAVELER   Yeah. (*The Traveler gets up from his wheelchair.*)

PAUL   You look good.

TRAVELER (*getting it, smiling*)   Yeah?

PAUL   Yeah.

The Traveler points to Paul's shirt, indicates with his hand that it is only so-so. Paul laughs.

This is a rehearsal tape you sent me once. Your song.

Paul and The Traveler sit on the floor. The voice on the tape sings a song the Traveler wrote.

VOICE   "In the middle of the path of life, I lost my way."

Paul encourages the Traveler to sing along

PAUL   "I lost my way . . ."

The Traveler makes small sounds, but gets almost no notes of the melody. He works at it, though.

TRAVELER   "Alaaaaaaaaaanhg ghaah paaaah . . ."

Aaron appears at the entrance of the solarium with his bag. He stops to watch.

VOICE   "And found myself in shadows, I found myself in a forest . . ."

The Traveler keeps trying. Aaron sits by them, sings too.

"And in the forest, it was night. In the forest, it was cold.
And I tremble now to speak of it, and feel close to dying."

The song is over. The Traveler's attention is caught by a speck in Aaron's eye. Paying careful attention, he cleans Aaron's eye with his finger. Then he notices that the tip of his finger is wet.

TRAVELER (*to Aaron*)   It's . . . "tear"?

Aaron nods yes. The Traveler looks at Aaron, puzzled.

AARON   It's a tear. Yes. It's okay. It's okay to cry, isn't it?

He touches the other two. For a moment the Traveler appreciates the closeness between the three of them. Then he can't stand it anymore and dives for the potato chips.

TRAVELER   It's sha sha.

Laughter. The tension is broken.

AARON (*to Paul*) Happy birthday. Have some sha sha.

Aaron hands Paul the chips. The Traveler has an abrupt mood change. He tells the story of the stroke moment again. Aaron and Paul pay full attention.

TRAVELER (*though unable to muster much affect, mimics the woman doctor in the operating room*) Ahhh, ahhh. Mistake. It's . . .

PAUL Whose mistake?

TRAVELER It's . . .

PAUL A doctor?

AARON (*a flash of intuition*) Right after I saw you wheeled away— something went wrong.

PAUL In the operating room? (*He mimes getting an injection.*)

TRAVELER (*trying to mimic again, still without much affect*) Ahhh. Ahhh.

AARON A doctor panicked?

TRAVELER Ahhh, ahhh.

PAUL The stroke.

The Traveler claps his hand over his mouth.

PAUL They gagged you?

TRAVELER (*a whispery sound, hand over mouth*) Ahhhhh . . .

PAUL You wanted to scream—

AARON Something was wrong. You wanted to stop the operation but you couldn't. Oh, God.

PAUL Jesus.

TRAVELER (*realizing they got it, angry at what happened*) Yeah. (*The Traveler limps off angrily, talking to himself.*) Hating every everythings. Feeling like bomb. (*Paul starts to follow.*)

AARON (*calling him back*) Paul.

PAUL What now?

AARON (*agitated, stuffing the party food back into his bag*) Nothing— nothing, nothing, nothing.

PAUL If somebody goofed—

AARON Maybe they goofed. Maybe they panicked. I don't know. He doesn't know. How do we know?

PAUL If they knew he could have a stroke during the operation, why didn't they do something?

AARON Do what?

PAUL Did they have to operate?

AARON He was in heart failure. He had five days to live.

PAUL Wasn't it up to him to decide?

AARON (*pulling himself together*) If he wanted to die he's had every chance. He wants to live.

PAUL We'll sue them for a hundred million dollars.

AARON That's up to him. Legal suits drag on. His anger could freeze, turn bitter. Look, I don't trust doctors. But he does. They saved his life five times, as Jodie keeps telling us. He needs his faith in doctors.

PAUL So what does he do now? What do we do?

AARON He goes on. And we help him.

They walk in the corridor.

PAUL Did they tell him a stroke was possible?

AARON No—but he had a premonition.

PAUL (*discouraged*) Can you imagine living with all this?

AARON Yes.

PAUL You're not who I expected.

AARON Don't tell me what your family says about me. I can imagine.

PAUL How long have you known him, anyway?

AARON Fifteen years in September. Gulp. You were two. I auditioned for him in a loft on Twenty-fourth Street. I sang "Blowin' in the Wind"—uptempo. It was not a good idea.

PAUL So how come you're here, even though . . .

AARON Even though we're not lovers now? Habit? Fear of being alone? Not knowing how to let go? There's no sane reason for loving a narcissist.

PAUL Is he a narcissist?

AARON We've been through open heart before—twice. After surgery he's vulnerable as a kitten, like now. Then as he gets better he turns mean again. I know what to expect.

PAUL If you know . . . ?

AARON It's choiceless. I have to muster all my wits, drop my own cuckoos—my hysteria, my self-pity—'cause there's no room for them now. What a relief—just to do what needs to be done.

PAUL But if—

AARON But if, but if, but if! Here. Happy birthday. (*Aaron hands Paul a wrapped present.*) Now scram.

Aaron kisses Paul on the cheek and shoves him gently on his way. Lights out on Aaron's side of the stage. The Traveler has reached his room, still angry. Jodie is there. The Traveler grabs her hand and pulls her to where his street clothes hang.

JODIE   What is it?

TRAVELER (*meaning "Let's get out—pronto"*)   Cashaprout—tonto.

The Traveler pulls out his worn canvas travel bag. Then he pulls his clothes down. As the Traveler throws down each thing, Jodie picks it up.

JODIE (*not sure how to handle this*)   What are you doing? Stop it. You can't leave. You can't leave. The doctor hasn't released you.

TRAVELER (*throwing things down*)   Yeah!

JODIE (*putting things back*)   Stop it. Your whole life—you've done just what you want to do. Stop it. You can't do what you want to do now. Stop it. You can't leave.

TRAVELER (*grabbing his bag back from her*)   Yeah? Because!

AARON (*appearing at the door*)   He's not a prisoner, Jodie. He wants to leave.

JODIE (*spinning on Aaron, angry*)   You think you're the only one who knows what he wants? I know what he wants. He just can't have what he wants, that's all.

TRAVELER (*still shoving things into his suitcase*)   Tonto!

AARON   He can leave.

JODIE (*outraged*)   No, he can't! It's not up to him. It's up to the doctor.

AARON (*heading for the phone*)   I'll call him.

TRAVELER (*fueling the fire, seeing that Aaron is on his side*)   Yeah. Because. Tonto!

JODIE (*stopping Aaron's hand on the phone*)   I'll handle this, Aaron. He's *my* brother. This is a family matter—family. The doctor says *my* brother will get better sooner if he stays here for therapy. Get it?

AARON But what about him? Don't you care what he wants? He obviously wants to leave. He wants to be an outpatient.

The Traveler is calming down while Jodie and Aaron continue fighting.

JODIE Well, he can't. I'll decide what's right for *my* brother. He can blame me. I'll be the heavy. I'm used to it.

AARON You can't make his decisions for him. You can't treat him like an idiot child, Jodie. He's not your child.

JODIE He's not yours either, Aaron.

AARON You can't lock him up. You can't suffocate him.

JODIE Do you know what "family" means? "Family"?

Jodie jabs her finger in Aaron's direction. There is a moment's pause.

AARON I think I do.

TRAVELER (*sighing, losing interest, tired*) Yeah . . . tonto . . .

JODIE (*furious, on her way out*) You know who's in control here— legally, right?

Aaron, knowing he must cool it, is silent. Jodie is at the door. She pokes her finger toward Aaron.

If I have to, I go to a lawyer—and you are out.

She leaves. Jodie and the Traveler are silent for a moment.

AARON You know you said "Tonto"? (*Kneeling by the bed, Aaron writes on a pad, and sings out.*) Hi-yo, Silver, and away!

TRAVELER (*reading from the pad*) Tonto.

AARON You read it! You read it!!

The Traveler takes in what happened, then shrugs as if it were nothing. Aaron laughs.

Yay, Lone Ranger.

Aaron kisses him. Dr. Steiff and Moira come in.

DR. STEIFF (*to the Traveler*) Jodie says you're getting restless. You know . . . there's a garden down there for patients . . . and, uh, the gate is open all afternoon, and . . .

Aaron grabs the Traveler's army surplus outdoor coat.

. . . if someone with a car were waiting by the gate . . . Well, as long as the patient just came and went in one afternoon . . .

Aaron and Moira are already preparing the Traveler to go out.

. . . Why, I wouldn't have to know anything about it, would I?

Dr. Steiff winks, and leaves with Moira.

AARON (*to the Traveler*) The garden gate?

Aaron excitedly hums the theme song of "The Lone Ranger" as he goes out. The Traveler, wearing his army coat, limps out of his room and into the garden.

TRAVELER (*to himself*) Refugee. Coming to frontier. Refugee to frontier—

Voices of children playing. The Traveler stops to listen.

It's children—Coming to children. It's Georgia—Home to Children.
Myself feeling to child. But can-not spitch to child.
Thinkin' 'bout that.

Aaron, wearing his jacket and hat, appears as if on the other side of a gate. The Traveler is delighted to see him, as if they hadn't met in a long time.

Hi!

The Traveler steps forward, as if over a frontier.

AARON Hi.

New York traffic noise as the scene changes to the Traveler's apartment. Aaron stands silently as the Traveler inspects his home. It has an empty look to it. The Traveler pretends to glance through a stack of mail on the worktable. He dusts off the answering machine, accidentally playing his own outgoing message. It sounds exactly as we heard him record it.

TRAVELER'S VOICE ON ANSWERING MACHINE Hi, I'm out. Please leave your number, and I'll call you back as soon as I possibly can.

The Traveler, shocked, backs away from the table, knocking up against the bookshelf. He is still for a moment, then decisive.

TRAVELER Krasha hospital.

The Traveler makes a decisive hand gesture, as if clearing away something he doesn't want.

Krasha.

He is refusing to return to the hospital. Aaron smiles, shrugs, helps the Traveler off with his coat.

AARON Okay.

TRAVELER It's to—exerse—mash to spitch, exerse—to work.

Dr. Sullivan arrives. Bach music plays during physical therapy, which we witness over several weeks. As the Traveler works, Aaron sets up the Traveler's apartment. He rearranges objects and papers on the worktable into neat piles, places a fresh flower in a bottle and puts labels on the bookshelves: "Anthropology," "Lear Opera," "Speech Therapy," "Aphasia" and "Slow Down!" He posts a large "Appointments Chart."

DR. SULLIVAN (*moving the Traveler's limbs*) Relax. Arms to side. Breathe in. Arms up. Breathe out. Good. Arms down. Breathe in. Arms up. Breathe out. Arms down. Breathe out. Good. Relax. Now up on the ball of the foot. And down. Good.

Dr. Sullivan is economical in her use of words to the Traveler. He is exercising in place. Paul arrives, sits on the floor, watches the Traveler.

TRAVELER (*wanting to say something about his right side*) Shalaff sha.

DR. SULLIVAN Breathe out—up on the ball of the foot. And down. Good. Now walk.

279

She indicates by touching his legs. He begins to walk.

TRAVELER To right—it's—

DR. SULLIVAN Hurts on the right—

TRAVELER Shalman . . .

DR. SULLIVAN The muscle groups are contracted.

TRAVELER (*continuing to explain*) Shaloman sha.

DR. SULLIVAN But you're walking better than you were. You're walking better.

Dr. Sullivan adjusts his right foot so that it points straight forward. Dr. Sullivan speaks to Paul and Aaron as she massages the Traveler's right leg, and helps him to walk.

Don't ask him to repeat your pronounciation. He has to retrieve words from his mind, and that's a subtle process. There's no prescribed way. Speech exercises may help, or they may not. We have to help him surprise himself into going around the blocked area in the brain.

Dr. Sullivan leaves. The Traveler continues exercising. Paul gives him a chair to steady himself. Aaron hands Paul some papers.

PAUL Okay. Homework. Remember menu, tip and appetizer? A list of food and prices is a—

TRAVELER Wantings tip.

PAUL Yeah, but—

TRAVELER Wantings tip. Wantings shamalsha.

PAUL You want a tip but that's not the point.

TRAVELER Myself tip. (*He mimes pocketing a tip.*) Myself shamalsha. (*He mimes eating the appetizer.*)

PAUL I know, but—

TRAVELER (*miming a blind man*)   Okay, okay, okay. Myself—

PAUL   Blind.

TRAVELER (*after making sure from Paul's tone that he got it*)   Good. (*The Traveler indicates being deaf.*) Myself—

PAUL   Deaf.

TRAVELER (*knowing from Paul's tone that he got it*)   Good. (*He mimes a beggar.*)

TRAVELER   Wantings tip.

Laughter from Paul and Aaron.

PAUL (*leaving*)   You win.

Dr. Sullivan comes in again.

DR. SULLIVAN (*watching the Traveler*)   Heel, toe. Heel, toe. (*She attempts to help him.*)

TRAVELER (*wanting to do it alone*)   Myself.

DR. SULLIVAN   Okay. Breathe in, arms up. Breathe out, arms down.

TRAVELER   Breathings . . .

DR. SULLIVAN   Good.

TRAVELER   Feeling to . . . ma-ashalom.

DR. SULLIVAN   I don't understand.

TRAVELER (*straining to say the word, frustrated*)   Ma, ma, ma-ashalm.

DR. SULLIVAN (*face-to-face with the Traveler*)   Wait. Slowly. Take it easy. It'll come if you relax. You're feeling like what?

TRAVELER   Because . . . Strong to body, krasha to speech—feeling to— (*The Traveler beats his chest.*)

AARON, DR. SULLIVAN   Tarzan!

DR. SULLIVAN (*leaving*)   See you tommorrow, Tarzan.

Jodie comes in wearing a raincoat.

TRAVELER (*making his gesture of wiping away*)   Krasha.

JODIE   I know, I get it.

TRAVELER (*angry but controlled*)   Krasha, yeah. Krasha, krasha Minipolice.

JODIE   I know. You won't come to Minneapolis.

TRAVELER   Yeah! Minipolice: yeah, yeah, yeah.

JODIE   I get it. I came to say good-bye.

TRAVELER (*leaving the room*)   Angle!

He leaves. We hear a door slam.

JODIE (*close to tears*)   What does "angle" mean?

AARON   "I have to lie down and watch TV."

JODIE   I was nineteen. I had made seven hundred and fifty dollars as a waitress. Seven hundred and fifty dollars was a lot. I wanted to go to college. Or business school. But Mama was worried to death about his heart, so there was his doctor and his trip to Georgia to the cardiac home . . . And now he hates me.

AARON   No he doesn't. It's a love ritual—it's family S and M. You love him, you crowd him, he kicks you away—you hurt, he feels guilty.

JODIE   How do you know so much about it?

AARON   We're in the same boat, Jodie. I'll get my walking papers too. My turn will come. I'd like to think not, but it will. Cross my heart and hope to die.

JODIE   So nothing's changed?

AARON I don't know. In a funny way, this crisis has made me see how strong I am. Maybe I can actually let go. For years now I've been hanging on to someone who uses me. I've hated myself, and not done him much good either. I'm middle-aged. I want to get my singing together. And just maybe I want to find someone else.

JODIE So who's going to take care of him?

AARON He is. With some help from all of us.

JODIE You think he can?

AARON I think he *will*—whether you and I like it or not. He has admirers. He can materialize anything he needs.

JODIE (*agreeing*) Yeah—my kid brother the star.

The Traveler comes out of his bedroom. Ignoring Jodie, he sits at his worktable.

JODIE (*to the Traveler*) Listen, I'm sorry . . .

Hesitantly Jodie reaches out to touch the Traveler. He sharply shakes away her hand.

JODIE So long, kid. I'll call you when I get to Minneapolis. So long, Aaron.

AARON Good-bye, Jodie.

Aaron and Jodie embrace. Jodie leaves. Aaron watches the Traveler as he grabs some ice cream, which he eats compulsively out of the container.

TRAVELER (*listing to Aaron what he cannot do*) Krasha to al-col. (*He demonstrates drinking.*) Krasha—(*He demonstrates smoking.*) Krasha, krasha. Must to *something*.
Sometime myself hating every everyones. Hating my-self. (*He paces.*) Good-bye, good-bye—to left. Feeling like that.
Every, every: difficult to hard—

AARON I made you something. (*Aaron unrolls a drawing of a human brain drawn on a map of the United States. He points.*) New York. Minneapolis.

TRAVELER (*his mood changing immediately*)   It's to humans' brain. Wow.

AARON   Yeah. As many roads in a brain as there are in America.

TRAVELER   Wow.

AARON   And then the stroke. (*Aaron demonstrates stroking.*)

TRAVELER   To stroke?

AARON   Something—maybe a piece of your old heart valve—traveled up to the brain. It blocked off some roads. (*Aaron demonstrates by blocking off a small area on the brain-map.*)

TRAVELER (*understanding, impressed*)   Detour.

AARON   Yeah. You need to learn detours now.

TRAVELER (*grateful for the map demonstration*)   Thinking of everythings. (*He looks at the brain-map.*) Wow, it's clear—it's true. (*He speaks about his own mind.*) Sometimes it's clear, the brain. Some seconds, it's perfects. It's true. (*He has an abrupt mood change.*) Sometime krasha. Forgetting—it's feeling to crazy.

AARON   No, you're not crazy. You're less crazy than before the stroke.

TRAVELER   A-phasia—it's word. (*The Traveler grabs the "Aphasia" sign from the bookcase and holds it to his chest.*) It's Greek: a-phasia. It's "rats." It's to cancer—Peoples running away—(*He demonstrates people running in fear.*) —"ahhh, ahhh."

AARON   People are afraid because they do not understand. You must help them.

TRAVELER (*looking in the mirror*)   Beginning looking to crazy.

AARON (*emphatically*)   You do not. You look nice.

TRAVELER (*pacing, angry*)   "Nice." It's terrible word.
Feeling to child—like that.
Sometime understandings nothing, nothings.
Working improv-e-ments—spitch—spitch—exercise, spitch—

Walking, mass-age . . . It's to school, it's child—okay, okay. If two months nothing improv-ements—good-bye, good-bye. (*Grabbing a letter opener, he mimes stabbing himself.*)

AARON (*not joking*)   How about giving it six months—six?

TRAVELER (*seeing that Aaron is disturbed*)   It's okay.

AARON   It's not okay with me.

TRAVELER (*with humor*)   Myself already to dead. Krasha to suicide. (*The Traveler, looking at papers on his worktable, smiles.*) It's—it's to . . . will. Good idea. It's . . . to Paul. (*He speaks Paul's name with love.*)

AARON (*excited*)   You said a name—name—"Paul"!

TRAVELER (*understanding*)   It's name?

AARON (*hugging him*)   Yeah.

TRAVELER   Wow. It's improv-e-ment. Slow improv-e-ment . . . but stroke—it's quick. It's— (*He demonstrates lightning.*)

AARON   Lightning. It's lightning.

TRAVELER   Yeah . . . to brain. Stroke, it's, of course—

AARON   Slowly.

TRAVELER   Stroke, it's curse. Everything puzzle—feeling like that now. But stroke, it's also— (*He mimes receiving something from heaven.*)

AARON   A blessing.

TRAVELER   Before stroke: only my-self, my-self. Now seeing more to . . . (*He grabs something red.*)

AARON   Seeing red?

The Traveler grabs something of another color.

Seeing more colors now.

TRAVELER (*picking up a speck of dust*)   More to shaloh . . . to small. (*The Traveler takes a hot pepper off his worktable.*) Loving to hot now, to pepper. It's true. (*He eats it.*)

AARON (*bites into one—gags*)   Wow—these really are hot.

The Traveler wrestles some ice cream into Aaron's mouth. Aaron reacts to the taste. They laugh, landing on the floor.

AARON   This morning—remember, when the coffee shop man asked, "Where are you from?" you said . . .

TRAVELER (*pleased to repeat it*)   Poland.

AARON   You know, I'm actually happy. I must have made twenty phone calls. But it's all arranged. We are actually driving to the mountains. Po-co-nos. The Poconos. Like Pocahontas. (*Aaron sings.*) "What a day this has been, what a rare mood I'm in . . ."

TRAVELER (*getting up, speaking quietly but determinedly*)   Krasha Po-co-nos myself.

AARON   What do you mean? As if I didn't know.

TRAVELER (*gesturing his "cannot"*)   Krasha Po-co-nos. Krasha Po-co-nos myself.

AARON   You don't want to go—again?

TRAVELER (*meaning Aaron should go alone*)   Yourself. Yourself. Krasha—myself.

AARON (*his anger rising*)   We've been all through this. We've been through it and through it. I asked you a month ago—one month. (*When Aaron speaks a number, he holds up the corresponding number of fingers.*) You said you wanted to go. I called around. I found a hotel near water, like you said: Nice view, nice folks—they sounded nice. Made a reservation for five days: Five. Then you said, "only three." Three. So I called back, made it three, rented a car, found someone to water my plants, your plants. Then last Sunday you say you're not going, so I cancel everybody. Then on Tuesday you say "okay," for two nights: two.

TRAVELER (*He didn't know then how he would feel now.*) I did-n't know.

AARON Okay, so I call them all back. It's on again, I say. Now you want me to cancel? Again? Is that right?

TRAVELER Must to spitch. Must.

AARON (*furious*) You can miss speech therapy for two fucking days!

TRAVELER Must to spitch every, every.

Aaron begs on his knees in front of the Traveler.

AARON Please, let's just go. Let's just leave it as it is, get into the car and drive to the Poconos. Please—just this one thing—for me. On my knees. No more phone calls.

TRAVELER Krasha! Must. My-self. Every, every—every day!

AARON (*angrily hitting the Traveler hard on his calf*) Oh, shit!

TRAVELER (*indignant, stepping back from Aaron*) Hit! Hit! Can-*not*. Can-*not* Po-co-nos—not! Not!

AARON (*amazed he has actually struck the Traveler*) I'm sorry.

TRAVELER (*stepping farther back, his fury still growing*) Not! Not! *Must* to spitch!

AARON I'm sorry I hit you. It just happened.

The Traveler is expressing his rage at everything.

TRAVELER Can-*not* Po-co-nos. *My*-self to call—*my*-self. *My*-self—must *my*-self. (*He is scrambling for the phone number in Aaron's bag.*) *My*-self to call. Can-*not* Poc-o-nos. Can-not. Can-*not*. Because. Because. *Must* to spitch. (*The Traveler moves fast around the apartment, attempts to use the phone.*)

287

AARON Now wait. We're just talking about a weekend.

TRAVELER Can-not. Spitch. *My*-self. Not. Not. Can-not. Po-co-nos.

AARON (*trying to calm him*) Come on, this is opera. Save it for the stage.

TRAVELER True. True. (*He points to where Aaron was on his knees.*) Opera *your*-self.

AARON (*quietly*) Touché.

TRAVELER *Your*-self. Not true *my*-self. *Can*-not. *Can*-not. *My*-self. To spitch. Must.

AARON (*worried for the Traveler's heart*) Okay. Okay. We won't go. I'll call.

TRAVELER (*no longer hearing, shouting*) Must *my*-self! Not. Not. Not. No!

Aaron tackles him, toppling them both.

AARON Hey! Calm down.

The Traveler struggles as they roll on the floor.

TRAVELER No, no, no!

AARON (*pinning him down, speaking calmly*) Well, you certainly learned to say "no."

The Traveler stops struggling. They remain on the floor.

AARON (*after a moment*) It's okay. We're not going. Do you know how come you can get so angry at me?

TRAVELER (*not quite giving up yet*) Must—

AARON Because I love you. Because I love you. And do you know why you're angry?

The Traveler is silent.

AARON Because you hate being dependent. Dependent—you hate it.

TRAVELER (*hesitantly, admitting it*) Yeah. (*He starts listing the many times in his life that he was ill.*) Asha to five, and asha to ten, again—

AARON (*interrupting him*) Yes. Each time you thought you'd die, but—

TRAVELER (*softly*) Hell.

AARON But now it's different, it's different—you've had a stroke, but—

TRAVELER Stroke—it's lightning to brain.

AARON Yes. But not to the heart. You don't have a heart problem now.

TRAVELER Difficult. Difficult to born . . .

AARON Yeah. Difficult for me too. (*Aaron gets up.*) I'm going home now. (*Aaron slips on his jacket and hat and grabs his bag.*) I have some songs to learn. Songs. I'm going on that tour.

TRAVELER You should. You must.

The Traveler kisses Aaron.

AARON Coming and going—it's okay?

TRAVELER It's okay.

Aaron leaves. The Traveler sits at his worktable.

Sentence. Hating sentence but must every every day. (*He reads from a piece of paper.*) "Take off your gloves, please." (*He puts the paper down.*) It's a sentence. (*He confides this with pride.*) Sentence: It's organization—
It's human organization.
From sen-tence to story—
It's mysterious, it's true.

Difficult when peoples changing to topic,
It's difficulty—it's true.
Difficult to numbers.
Wri-ting to appoint-ments—whew!
But can to read. It's funny. (*He picks up a book from the table, and reads aloud from it slowly, paying careful attention to meaning.*) "Chinese-speaking people who have had a stroke have an easier time than English-speaking people. That is because Chinese is stored on the right side of the brain, while the English language, along with arithmetic, is stored on the left side of the brain." China: it's one quarter to earth—wow.
Thinkin' 'bout that . . . (*He picks up a piece of paper.*) New-row-logist, it's fortune-teller to brain. (*He points to what is written on the paper.*) "Six months: much improvements." That's all. "One years: less improvements." That's all.
Putting curse! (*He crumples the paper, throws it away.*)
Brain, it's mysterious.
Brain, it's—it's universe, it's stars—to Einstein.
It's true. (*He reads from a newspaper clipping.*) "New Evidence Points to Growth of Brain Even Late In Life."
It's *New York Times*—it's true.
Beethoven to stroke, then to music more.
Every, every sound like new.
Every word like new—feeling like that.
Like baby—New word: wow, wow.
Myself feeling "word": wow.
But sentence, it's different. Sentence, it's—(*He reads from his notebook.*) "Civilization." (*He's impressed by this word.*) It's a sentence. (*He reads from his notebook.*) "How are you?" "I am okay." (*He puts down the notebook.*) It's a sentence: coming to earth. (*He picks up his flute, comes downstage and plays the few notes of melody he heard in his surgery dreams. Then shyly, still with difficulty enunciating, he introduces himself to the audience. We hear his name for the first time.*) I am a composer.
My name is Daniel.

He stands for a moment. Lights out.